I0800974

The McGowan Trilogy

Praise for *The McGowan Trilogy*

Many have written about the situation in the North of Ireland – few with such gusto and attention to detailed violence as Scanlon. There are shades of Joe Orton and Martin McDonagh in these plays but Scanlon ploughs his own bloody, uproarious furrow.

– Larry Kirwan (*Hard Times*), black47.com

A trio of plays that begins with comedy and irreverence and ends with pathos and loss, Séamus Scanlon's *The McGowan Trilogy* is surprising, original and hugely enjoyable.

– Christian O'Reilly (*Chapatti*), theagency.co.uk

The McGowan Trilogy is a superb achievement. Addictive in its telling, the 3 sections come together to plot points on a map that is part a man's soul and part a hell of his own creation. Wonderfully done by Séamus Scanlon, *The McGowan Trilogy* opens a pandora's box of ambition and regret, and in the process leaves the viewer haunted.

– Urban Waite (*Sometimes the Wolf*), urbanwaite.com

The McGowan Trilogy tells the story of psychopath, street–wise philosopher and executioner, Victor McGowan, and those unfortunates who come within his orbit. O'Casey meets Behan, both on LSD with a little bit of Guests of the Nation thrown-in for good measure. Incisive wit, gallows humor and intelligent one-liners. Powerful and original, right to the last.

– Sam Millar (*On the Brinks*), millarcrime.com

What a delight for fans of Scanlon's terrific noir fiction to see him put his verbal virtuosity and storytelling flair to theatrical use! With its crackling dialogue and bravura blend of black comedy and unnerving violence, *The McGowan Trilogy* shares some dramatic DNA with the work of both Martin McDonagh and Quentin Tarantino. It possesses, however, an emotional, often poetic, power all its own. At its center stands a wholly original creation, an Irish revolutionary with a ferocious intelligence, a savage sense of humor, and – for all his ruthlessness – a very human capacity for guilt, grief, and confusion.

– Harold Schechter *(The Mad Sculptor)*, haroldschechter.com

Dancing at Lunacy is psychotic vaudeville from the pen of a punk rock Pinter, a gory, hilarious fairground ride to the dark side

– Paul Duane (*Barbaric Genius*), www.screenworks.ie

The McGowan Trilogy is heart-stoppingly dark and gloriously poetic.

– SJ Rozan (*Ghost Hero*), sjrozan.net

Séamus Scanlon's *The McGowan Trilogy,* set on both sides of the porous Irish border during the 'troubles' of the 1980s, is internecine both in the modern sense (relating to internal struggles) as well as the word's original meaning (fought all the way to the death). Scanlon's literate theatricality is devastating but irresistible.

– James L. de Jongh (*Vicious Modernism*)

Victor McGowan in *The McGowan Trilogy* is a charming psycho, the bastard child of Samuel Beckett and Quentin Tarantino. He's the kind of character you're compelled to make a big song and dance about. And he'd be sure to join in, offering you his last Tayto crisp with one hand while shooting you in the head with the other.

– Al Guthrie *(The Abandoned),* www.allanguthrie.co.uk

The McGowan Trilogy is filled with music and murder, melancholy and regret. Victor McGowan, Scanlon's protagonist, demonstrates the chilling way that – in John Cale's immortal words – 'the waster and the wasted get to look like one another in the end'. Strong stuff, dark and bitter as the past.

– Joseph Goodrich (*The Red Box*), playscripts.com/playwrights

Scanlon is a bloody fine storyteller and a truly imposing writer. *Dancing at Lunacy*'s fierce and unflinching combination of tragedy, absurdity and wit set him apart.

– Peter A. Quinn *(Dry Bones),* newyorkpaddy.com

Dancing at Lunacy is a sharp, super-charged punk-rock driven IRA drama that is dark, chaotic, button-pushing and resonant. Scanlon's dialogue combines nasty wit, poetry and blasphemy.

– Jonathan Santlofer (*The Death Artist),* jonathansantlofer.com

The McGowan Trilogy's Victor is an unforgettable character. He is an Irish Hannibal Lecter – supremely dangerous, sophisticated, and totally literate. Séamus Scanlon's prose flows off Victor's lips in an unending alliterative stream of dark images and word play. Victor is a psychopathic killer whose erudition makes him one of the most disturbing characters I have read about in a long time.

– Steven Simring, MD, Clinical Associate Professor of Psychiatry,
Columbia University College of Physicians and Surgeons

Séamus Scanlon

THE MCGOWAN TRILOGY

Three Inter-Related One Act Plays

ARLEN
HOUSE

The McGowan Trilogy

is published in 2014 by
ARLEN HOUSE
42 Grange Abbey Road
Baldoyle
Dublin 13
Ireland
Phone/Fax: 353 86 8207617
Email: arlenhouse@gmail.com
arlenhouse.blogspot.com

Distributed internationally by
SYRACUSE UNIVERSITY PRESS
621 Skytop Road, Suite 110
Syracuse, NY 13244–5290
Phone: 315–443–5534/Fax: 315–443–5545
Email: supress@syr.edu

978–1–85132–111–7, paperback

Typesetting by Arlen House
Printed lithographically in Dublin
Front cover image by Serge Nivelle

Contents

The McGowan Trilogy: A Serial in Three Acts, was incubated by The Cell Theater Company, Ltd., and first performed at **the cell**, A Twenty First Century Salon™, NYC, NY on 11 September 2014.

ARTISTIC AND DESIGN
Nancy Manocherian – Founding Artistic Director
Kira Simring – Director
Séamus Scanlon – Playwright
Brian Reager – Assistant Director
Siena Zoe Allen – Costume Designer
Dylan Fusillo – Sound Designer
Gertjan Houben – Scenic/Lighting Designer
Samantha Keogh – Dramaturgy/Prop Designer
Jed Peterson – Fight Choreographer

STAGE MANAGEMENT
Mackenzie Meeks – Production Manager
Rachel Kitto – Stage Manager
Anne Ciarlone – Assistant Stage Manager

CAST
Paul Nugent* – Victor McGowan
Cindy Boyle* – May McGowan
Philip Callen* – Pender
Matt Golden* – Ahern
Conor McIntyre – Barman
Anna Nugent* – Woman
*These actors appeared courtesy of Actors' Equity Association. An Equity Approved Showcase.

Dancing at Lunacy was incubated by The Cell Theater Company, Ltd., and first performed at **the cell**, A Twenty First Century Salon™, NYC, NY in March 2012 with:
Paul Nugent – Victor McGowan
Phil Callen – Pender
Todd Pate – Ahern
Brett Arasco – Barman
Ciaran Byrne – Doyle
Spencer Leopold-Cohen – Bar Customer

Nancy Manocherian

FOUNDING ARTISTIC DIRECTOR'S INTRODUCTION

The first time I met Séamus Scanlon was at a gathering at **the cell**, my secret dream that lay dormant for years, until I, a playwright, met director Kira Simring. Having worked on a theater project together, she and I joined forces to make dreams come true; both ours and those of many unrecognized artists.

It was early in the new century that **the cell**, a Twenty First Century Salon™ was opened to artists of many disciplines to incubate all kinds of new projects.

On Sundays, we hosted a 'literary salon', curated by Karen Heuler, a teaching writer whose class I had attended at NYU. She had good instincts for choosing writers to read excerpts from their new works.

It was Sunday afternoon. Séamus read. I listened. He was funny, wise, wry, twisted and dead serious about killing. He was also seriously talented. How could a little story about an assassin make me laugh and cry in one phrase? I was intrigued. Listening to him read, I felt the way I always hoped to feel when approaching a novel, film, play or any work of art; I was moved. Blown away, actually. And so was everyone there.

At the end of the reading, Séamus and I spoke. I think I let him know that we primarily incubated plays and perhaps could help him if he had one, but had no connection to the publishing world. Some weeks later, Séamus submitted *Dancing at Lunacy* which he had transformed from a short story into ... a play!

I read it. I was so excited by the prospect of presenting his play, I immediately handed it to Kira, hoping she would love it too. She did. Very quickly and excitedly we went about incubating *Dancing at Lunacy* as a one-act play.

Finding the right leading man would be key to the play's success. I searched the Rolodex of my mind and remembered a cute Irishman we had seen years before. I had a feeling. I could recall his dimpled smile and the circumstances of our meeting, but not his name. He was the husband of an actor, Anna Nugent, whose sister, Naomi Olson, was a friend of Kira's from an earlier life as a barista.

Thankfully, as with many cell-centric affairs, Kira's great memory along with providence intervened to bring Séeamus and Paul Nugent together. A match made in heaven.

Séamus found his lovable scoundrel in Paul. We were on a roll with our one-act. Directed by Kira Simring and starring Paul Nugent as Victor McGowan, *Dancing at Lunacy* was an instant success as Séamus simultaneously received literary awards for his short stories.

As our relationship with Séamus grew, his playwriting expanded. I felt his stories would work well as a serial, so we decided to try something new. Much to our delight, his outstanding trilogy is being published by Arlen House as we present it, in serial form.

In addition, Paul's wife, Anna Nugent, the sister of Kira's old friend, Naomi, will play alongside Paul. **The cell** salon is flourishing as a home for artists.

True to our mission, we proudly present *The McGowan Trilogy,* a work to mine the mind, pierce the heart and awaken the soul.

Kira Simring

Artistic Director's Introduction

I don't like violence – but Victor McGowan does. He's the protagonist of the plays you're about to read and I'm about to direct. Nancy Manocherian, the Founding Artistic Director of **the cell**, chose to feature *The McGowan Trilogy* as part of the First Irish Theatre Festival this year.

I've never held a gun, punched anyone, or been pistol-whipped. The closest I've been to a fight was a karate match when I was 8 and a self-defense class when I was 16. I don't have the stomach to watch torture, brutality, or physical violence. I close my eyes and cover my ears during the scary parts of movies (and books). But Séamus isn't writing violence; he's writing in response to it.

McGowan is a monster, but the world is a more potent monster. No one likes to admit it, but it's difficult to maintain one's humanity. Virtue isn't rewarded and life is cruel.

Victor McGowan has traded his humanity for an ideological commitment and each play in this trilogy challenges his ability to maintain this perverse stoicism.

Paul Nugent is the ideal actor to embody McGowan because he is the opposite of him. He feels deeply and cares about everyone. Paul plays the monstrous McGowan with absolute conviction and is powerfully convincing, and yet he is trustworthy. His portrayal subtly reveals McGowan's traumatized context, and so we empathize when he falters. We all know the world is a brutal place, even though we close our eyes and cover our ears.

Paul Nugent

Lead Actor's Introduction

Ok, I admit it, I'm in love with a sociopath. No, I don't mean writer Séamus Scanlon (though I'm pretty sure he's done some assassinations) or director Kira Simring (though she is definitely a ninja) or producer Nancy Manocherian (though she is certainly on America's Most Wanted list). I'm talking about Victor M. McGowan.

The love affair started by chance. Or let's be romantic. By kismet. You know how it goes.

You move to New York and your sister-in-law who lives in Hawaii says she used to work in a cafe in the Castro in San Francisco with this chick who is now a director in the city and you should meet and you do and it goes pretty well as she and her producing-partner are clearly cool and ambitious and smart but then you don't hear from her for years and then suddenly she calls out of the blue and says she's got this whacky short story writer from Galway who has written a play and her producer-partner remembered that odd Irish boy who they met and maybe he should come play the part in a little reading and you read the script and the play is exhilarating and action-packed and funny like a shark grinning and with a palpable break-the-rules vibrancy and a cutting bravery you just don't find in most plays and your heart starts racing and you speak the first line and all of a sudden this voice comes out and its not yours but it's kind of funny and kind of scary and really exciting, and you know, right then, that you've fallen in love. You know, the usual.

And of course, the first part of the relationship is all the sexy stuff. You do this play now called *Dancing at Lunacy* at **the cell** on West 23rd Street, where McGowan investigates a possible informer in his beloved IRA ranks in a claustrophobic Belfast bar, with an ace cast and a whip-smart crew and sharp designers, not to mention the lucid guidance of a director and a producer who *get* it and *love* it, and every performance is a blast.

You find that this person is funny and cocky and quick-witted and adorable and tough and rebellious and principled (in a way). He loves music like his very heartbeat, whether it is Grace Jones, The Sex Pistols or a long-lost entry to the Eurovision Song Contest, likes to sing (though he can't help changing the lyrics) and his form of relaxation is that well-known dance, the pogo, which involves lots of jumping up and down in one place to the beat and flicking your head at its apex. He's a little OCD, and one hell of a disciplinarian, and is very particular about little things like how to make a cup of tea or the appropriate use of grammar or what potato snacks your bar sells.

Oh, yes, and he has a tendency to punch people and break their fingers. And to rip open their weak-points. And he's not even averse to cold-blooded murder.

So every night with him is just great fun, even if you might feel a little guilty afterwards. And then it's over, and while you feel so lucky to have those memories and that *Huffington Post* review and much stronger calves from all that pogoing, you already miss him.

Except he won't go away. He keeps hanging around. With those glaring eyes and that murderous pout. Séamus keeps turning up with more pages, more scenes, more one-acts with this guy. Sweet, you think. Only this is where the relationship gets tougher.

For two years, we wandered across New York, reading new scenes of McGowan. Now this guy who didn't seem to have a care in the world, who walked on fire and didn't burn, who appeared to be indomitably ice-cold, who seemed not just to be indifferent to killing but actually to revel in it, suddenly reveals something else. A heart. A brooding heart. A breaking heart. He isn't just in a room with a bunch of tough guys anymore. He's alone with women who know things about him. Who know where the cracks are. Where it's no joke anymore and death is calling in its chips and Victor is still holding that silver Colt. Wait, a second, maybe this guy is for real and maybe he has a genuine soul under all that devilish sneering bravado, and the years are showing their strain and their scars and their lessons and now he's in the midst of a tragedy where the walls are closing in and the night is dark out there.

We read the new scenes at great writers' groups like the INKubator at Jersey City's Arthouse, until we find that need to face an audience. Up in a Bronx Irish pub, we try out a new scene where a mysteriously on-the-run near-broken McGowan sneaks into the nursing home where his Alzheimered mother is, and you see hard-grown men in the audience with damp in their eyes. It's called *Boys Swam Before Me.* At the NEWvember Festival in upstate New York we do a rehearsed reading of a new one-act called *The Long Wet Grass* where McGowan has kidnapped someone who has broken the rules and so has to be executed. Only this time that person is his childhood sweetheart. (And I get to read it with my favourite actress in the world, the brilliant Anna Nugent, my wife). And when we read it, the theatre is quiet as a chill graveyard with tension and despair.

And then you knew you had something more. Something we needed to bring home to **the cell**.

Suddenly this isn't just a guilty thrill ride, letting you in on the black comic psychosis of regulated violence. Now you have a character with deep and surprising dimension, with history and weakness and a wavering hand, in a three-act story that is harshly meaningful and delicately powerful and may be a new classic, on a journey to hell like a rain-slicked snarling Hamlet crossed with Richard Stark's Parker, with Dostoyevsky's bloody hands, the Ulster punk attitude of the Undertones, and the black, bruised and beautiful Irish poetry only Séamus Scanlon could write.

So yeah, that's this play. This hilarious yet crushing trilogy of haunting death, the deadly need to prove oneself, and ultimate regret. This 'love-song of killing that cannot be undone', to quote the man himself.

You'll see why now I'm even more in love with Victor M. McGowan, even as he thrills and terrifies me.

The only thing is I'm not sure if Victor loves me back.

Can he …?

– New York, July 2014

Paul Nugent is an actor from Dublin, who originated the role of McGowan in Séamus Scanlon's *The McGowan Trilogy* at **the cell** in New York City.

Play Performing Rights

Application for the performing rights to this play must be made to:

Séamus Scanlon
Email: seamus.scanlon@gmail.com

who, upon payment of a fee, will issue a licence for the performance to be given. No performance may be given unless this licence has first been obtained.

THE McGOWAN TRILOGY

I

Dancing at Lunacy

Pre-Show Music (*Provisional*)

You Were Born To Die, Blind Willie McTell
Nadine, Chuck Berry
You Really Got Me, The Kinks
Heroes, David Bowie
As Close As You'll Ever Be, The Boomtown Rats

Characters:

VICTOR: Head of IRA Internal Security, male (late 20s/early 30s)

AHERN: IRA operative, male (40s)

PENDER: ASU IRA commander, male (50s)

BARMAN: Civilian (20s)

DOYLE: IRA driver (any age, off-screen voice)

Curtain up.

MUSIC: *'Bang a Gong (Get it On)' by* T Rex.

SETTING:
13 October 1984, day. Drinking club in Belfast, basement. AHERN *drinking at a table at ease reading paper with 'Brighton Bombing' on the front page. There are assorted books of Irish poetry and history. Behind the counter are various snacks for sale: bars of chocolate, crisps, Barry's Tea. Calendar on wall with picture of Bobby Sands.* BARMAN *stands behind counter reading book. On bar counter there is a radio playing 'Bang a Gong (Get it On)' by* T Rex. *Bottles of beer on counter. Empties on tables. A few on the floor. On the walls are posters of 'Love is a Battlefield'* (Pat Benatar*), 'As Close As You'll Ever Be'* (Boomtown Rats*), Pearse, Connolly, the Irish Proclamation, Hunger Strikers. Then front door buzzer sounds –* BARMAN *lowers volume of radio, puts book down (annoyed because of interruption), checks video monitor, fidgets with it, taps it a few times, irritated, then hits the intercom.*

BARMAN: *(Irritated*). Yes? Yes?

VICTOR: *(Off stage).* Yes yourself.

BARMAN: Who's there? The video is on the blink.

VICTOR: You're on the fucking blink. Typical. Nothing really works in IRA-land. Apart from me.

BARMAN: (*Hesitant*). So who's there?

VICTOR: *(Off stage).* Victor *is anam dom.* (*Beat*). That's Irish.

BARMAN: What?

VICTOR: (*Off stage*). Victor is my name, as in Victor M. McGowan. (*Beat*). Before you ask M stands for Murder.

BARMAN: (*Startled*). Wait – WHAT?

AHERN *looks up amused.*

VICTOR: *(Off stage).* M's for murder – that's a film – sorta.

BARMAN: Here what are you talking about?

VICTOR: *(Off stage).* The fillum – 'Dial M for Mother Fucking Murder' – Hitchcock like.

BARMAN: Here, I'm, I'm getting confused.

VICTOR: You're *summa cum laude* already.

BARMAN: Is that more Irish?

VICTOR: No – it's fucking Latin.

AHERN *moves to bar. Points finger to head to signify* VICTOR *is a headcase.*

VICTOR: Jesus you a Brit spy? You should know some Irish at this stage. Never mind. I am losing the will to live.

BARMAN: Do you know him?

AHERN: Yeah I do – he's away a lot – that's why you don't know him.

BARMAN: You can vouch for him so?

AHERN: Well I'm telling you I know him. You can't vouch for anyone in this game – it's your call.

BARMAN: I don't know what to do – I'm trying to follow protocol.

AHERN: Don't be asking me so. That is not protocol.

BARMAN *retrieves ring binder from under the counter which has protocols, hesitatingly checking page.*

VICTOR: *(Off air).* What the fuck's going on in there – is there some kind of kangaroo court – because that would be *très ironic*. Are you taking a vote – are you trying to decide? (*sings 'if I am naughty or nice' – as in song 'Santa Claus is Coming to Town').*

BARMAN: Where you from?

VICTOR: *(Off stage).* I am from around. Where the fuck are YOU from?

BARMAN: *(More authoritatively).* I'm the one asking the questions here.

VICTOR: *(Off stage).* You certainly are. *(Beat).* And you ask them so well.

BARMAN: *(Less assured).* So where you from then?

VICTOR: The Springfield Road – you know, as in the rifle, which is what I will ram up your arse if you don't open this door now.

BARMAN: Jesus. I don't really know you.

VICTOR: *(Off stage).* My psychiatrist says the same thing. Well boss, if you open the door maybe you'll get to know me.

BARMAN: I never heard your name around these here parts before.

VICTOR: *(Off stage).* Well that means I'm doing my job sorta. *(Beat).* I'm new. (*Long beat*). All shiny and new.

BARMAN *looks around for inspiration.* BARMAN *gestures with open arms like pleading – has no clue here.*

BARMAN: (*to* AHERN): What do you think?

AHERN: (*Shrugs).* Sure – I'd say you are safe enough.

Buzzer sounds again.

BARMAN: (*Frustrated. Long beat).* Look do you know Séamus Cryan?

VICTOR: *(Off stage).* Cryan, dyin' – open the door. It's the IRA. I haven't got all night – these dum-dum bullets are rustin' in the rain. (VICTOR *starts singing to air of former Eurovision Song Contest Entry 'Walking the Streets in the Rain' by* Butch Moore*).*

My poor heart feels like breaking
'Cause I'll never see you again
Still, nobody knows I am dyin'
'Cause I'm walking the streets in the rain
My tears are mixed through the raindrops
And I feel like I can't stand the pain
Still, nobody knows I am dying
'Cause I'm walking the streets in the rain.

AHERN: (*amused).* He's not going away you know?

VICTOR: (*Pounds the door and yells*). Open this fucking door – if the Brits spot me you'll be hanging by your scrawny neck from a lamppost on the Falls until you are dead, dead, dead. VICTOR: *(To the air of 'Grease')*.

Dead is the word
Is the word
It's got groove
It's got meaning
Dead is the time
Is the place
Is the motion
Dead is the way you'll be feeling.

AHERN: (*to* BARMAN). Open the door for fuck sake – he's doing my head in.

The BARMAN *opens the door by pressing intercom buzzer.* VICTOR *enters. Door bangs. He saunters down the steps humming to himself and carrying hold-all.* VICTOR *jumps last few steps. He mimics as if dismounting from Olympic parallel bar exercise or similar.* AHERN *watches amused.*

VICTOR: Degree of difficulty high. A 10. A Comaneci. A perfect score. Ireland's first gold medal in gymnastics. (*Beat*). Or anything. (*He looks around the drinking club. He puts the black hold-all on the ground.* AHERN *nods in greeting but* VICTOR *ignores him and strides past and crosses to the barcounter.* VICTOR *walks to the end of the bar upstage.* BARMAN *flinches when* VICTOR *slaps one hand on bar loudly making noise*). Jesus it's pissing out there.

BARMAN: Sorry about that like.

VICTOR: You can't help the weather sure. Even God can't do much about it. All he can do is cry which just adds to the precipitation. The Irish weather is a five star fucker! It would drive anyone to drink never mind poor sops like the Irish. It develops a melancholia supernova all over the land. Covering the living and the dead. The weather is responsible for more deaths than the poor old maligned IRA.

BARMAN: *(Bewildered looking).* Right. I meant the other – the extra security questions.

VICTOR: No bother. No bother.

BARMAN: Ok.

VICTOR: *(Sternly, hits countertop with the flat of his hand staring at the* BARMAN*).* Ok NOTHING! Never open the door unless you can see who it is. Follow protocol. Get that fucking video monitor fixed. *(Pointing at video monitor. Beat).* Who'd you think I was by the way?

BARMAN: I don't know – you could have been anyone.

VICTOR: Could I have been a Jehovah's Witness do you think?

BARMAN: *(Unsure).* Ah ... Maybe, I suppose.

VICTOR: Well they travel in pairs so they won't get lost in housing estates or be converted back to Catholicism by the local papists in the Falls and they wear stupid suits (*points at himself*) – is that me?

BARMAN: (*Reluctantly*). Well no.

VICTOR: Well then. *(Beat).* Could I have been a Prod?

BARMAN: I don't know.

VICTOR: What do you mean you don't know?

BARMAN: Well I suppose you could be.

VICTOR: Why the fuck would a Prod come down here unless he had a death wish?

BARMAN: I don't know.

VICTOR: Jesus, you don't know much do you? And don't say I don't know.

BARMAN: No but ...

VICTOR: *(Shouts).* Could I have been a Moonie?

BARMAN: *(Quickly).* No.

VICTOR: Could I have been a loonie?

BARMAN: *(Quickly).* What?

VICTOR: Trick question! *(Quickly).* How about a Hare-Krishna?

BARMAN: *(Quickly).* No!

VICTOR: *(Quickly).* Mountbatten?

BARMAN: *(Quickly).* No. But.

VICTOR: But nothing. It doesn't matter who I was. You shouldn't let anyone in unless you know them. Even the Pope. Ignore them.

BARMAN: I thought you just said ...

VICTOR: Don't mind what I just said. Just do your job. Keep that door closed to fuck and don't let anyone else in unless I tell you different.

BARMAN: Ok.

VICTOR: *(Appeased).* That way we can all live happily never after. (*Beat*). Where you get this bar counter – it's rather elegant old chap *(in feigned upper class English accent)* for a lowly drinking club. *(*VICTOR *runs his hands along the countertop as if caressing it. He bends down to the level of the top of the counter and with eyes at that level he watches his hand move along the top. He starts moving bottles and glasses out of the way as if tidying etc).*

BARMAN: *(Looking perplexed*). We got it after the Apollo Bar was bombed. It's the only thing that survived.

VICTOR: I'm not surprised. It's teak or something. (*Slaps counter*). Just like your head! (*Beat*). Only joking! (VICTOR *slowly climbs up on the counter and lies on his back. He mimics back stroke. He moves the length of the bar counter. Sings quietly to himself).*

Teak is the word
is the word
is the word
its got grooves
its got grow-th rings.

BARMAN *and* AHERN *exchange glances – do headcase signs.*

VICTOR: Aah my aching back. I may have lumbago. Lying in the long wet grass all night will do that. Fuck. (*Beat*). Ahh. This is ideal orthopaedic support. I could lie here for hours. I used to lie on the timber boat slips of Callow Lake waiting for high tide so I would float off the dock and into the water in a slow continuous flow. I would drift all night watching the stars.

VICTOR: *(Closes his eyes. Beat. After a few seconds he sits up suddenly).* Is this fucken bar open or what is the story?

BARMAN: (*On edge*). Yeah yeah – we are open. (*Beat. Unsure of himself*). Observe a customer before you. (*Points*).

VICTOR: Observe a customer before me is it? How very droll.

BARMAN: Ok, sorry. No offence. I am a bit nervous. I am not sure what to be saying.

VICTOR: When in doubt say nowt. You will live longer. *(Twists his back and neck. Sighs).* Aah – that is better.

BARMAN: What will you have so?

VICTOR: I'll have a cup of Barry's tea.

BARMAN: What?

VICTOR: A cup of Ireland's favourite tea, blended for the discerning Irish palate, if memory serves me and it should since I have total recall. *(Beat).* Did you know Ireland has the highest per capita intake of tea apart from Somosaland or someplace?

BARMAN: No I didn't know that. *(Beat. Hesitates).* Very droll!

VICTOR *stares at him.*

BARMAN: *(Swallows, then hesitatingly).* We don't have any tea.

VICTOR: What type of an establishment is this?

BARMAN: Well it's a drinking club.

VICTOR: And is tea not a drink?

BARMAN: Well I suppose it is but …

VICTOR: (*Feigning rage – slaps bar counter with hand*). I'll handle this. (VICTOR *goes as if to pull a gun from inside his jacket adopting a classic firing stance –* BARMAN *flinches – then with a big flourish* VICTOR *pulls out a tea bag*).

BARMAN: (*Ducks*). Jesus Christ! Fuck!

VICTOR: Here Mister Barman I always carry a few. (VICTOR *sings to the air of Mister Sandman*).

Mister Barman, someone to hold

Would be so peachy before we're too old

So please turn on your magic beam

(VICTOR *points at kettle*).

Mister Barman, bring me

Please, please, bring me

Mister Barman, bring me my tea.

BARMAN *takes teabag, wipes brow, looks around for kettle etc.*

VICTOR: It's ok, I'm only fucking with yer brain. If you have one. Joke – Jesus. Lighten up. Everyone is so sensitive these days. Put on the kettle so. (*Beat*). Also garsoon (*with sarcastic emphasis*) while the kettle is boiling can you pour me a glass of water that you haven't pissed into – if it isn't too much bother. (*Beat*). I like to stay pure.

BARMAN: Pure ok – no bother, no bother.

BARMAN *puts glass of water in front of* VICTOR. VICTOR *holds glass up to the light and inspects it. He wipes something from the lip of the glass and puts it down in disgust on the countertop.* BARMAN *dusts off kettle. Not sure how to proceed. Opens it – looks in. Pours water from large jug.*

VICTOR: (*In a rage*). What the fuck are those? (*He points at the snack displays*).

BARMAN: (*Startled*). What? What? Where?

VICTOR: There. Are you fucken blind?

BARMAN: These? (*Points at Toblerones*).

VICTOR: No not the Toblerones. What could be wrong with them? They are sexy sure. With the triangular packaging and all. And the colour. Look there. Beside them!

BARMAN: The Wa ... Walker's Crisps. These?

VICTOR *nods.* BARMAN *hands a pack to* VICTOR.

VICTOR: These are fucken Brit crisps. Are you a patriot or not? This country is totally fucked. Next you will be showing tennis from Wimbledon and cricket matches from Lords. (VICTOR *smashes the Walker's crisps bag on the counter multiple times with his palm. He throws away the shattered crisps bag. Crisps fly all over the stage).* Don't sell that shit anymore. Only sell Tayto. Tayto are your only man. Tayto are the real thing. (*He dances and sings 'You make me feel mighty real' by* Sylvester*).* Repeat after me.

BARMAN: (*Sings).* 'You make me feel mighty ...'

VICTOR: No. Not the fucken song. Mother of Jesus – give me patience. Tayto are your only man, ok?

BARMAN: Tayto are your only one.

VICTOR: Are your parents first cousins? Your only man it is I said. Not your only one. Fuck – close enough I suppose. Read Flann O'Brien when you graduate to a stay in the H-Blocks. (VICTOR *stretches, yawns then turns up radio on counter top. Music: 'One Way or Another' by* Blondie. VICTOR *nods to music – sways slightly – closes eyes. Lowers volume).* Deadly music this – what station is it?

BARMAN: Falls FM16.

VICTOR: I like it – great gun pun – glad there is someone around the Falls Road apart from myself with a functional brain stem. (*Then he sits down opposite* AHERN *and starts reading* AHERN*'s paper with mock interest. He begins to slowly pull down the pages until he is looking at* AHERN).

AHERN: *(Irritated but being solicitous).* Well McGowan? (B*eat).* I haven't seen you for years – you were away I suppose?

VICTOR: *(sings to tune of 'Away in a Manger')*

Away in big danger
no crib for a bed
the little IRA Victor
shot Brits in the head.
What's it to you anyway?

AHERN: Nothing. Small talk is all only. (*Beat*). Anyway I know. (*Points at 'BRIGHTON BOMBING' headlines on paper*).

VICTOR: (*Sighs).* This whole town is sieving like a leak.

AHERN: Sure. You came close though. (*Beat*). How'd you miss her?

VICTOR: I don't know. It was 3am. She should have been in bed. She was up reading or taking a shite or something. A shoite in time saves nine they say or something.

AHERN: Aye something. Sure we'll get her some time. As Danny Morrison says Thatcher has to be lucky all the time – we only have to be lucky once.

VICTOR: Just like here.

AHERN: What?

VICTOR: (*Indifferent).* Nothing. (VICTOR *walks around inspecting the posters on the walls. He stands in profile beside a poster of Padraic Pearse who is also in profile).*

AHERN: Re-incarnation time!

VICTOR: It's not really me – Pearse only lived to die – he was in love with the bullet symphony and rifle diphthongs.

AHERN: Classical music illusions. You are full of surprises.

VICTOR: It's allusions not illusions. Surprise is my middle name.

AHERN: As well as M for Murder!

VICTOR: You don't miss much.

AHERN: Well if it is not 'classified' can I ask how it's going with yourself?

VICTOR: To hell. The usual.

AHERN: I see.

VICTOR: Same place as you.

AHERN: What? You're a bit of a drama queen aren't you?

VICTOR: Well I am an MFA after all.

AHERN: What's that when it's at home?

VICTOR: Master of Fine Arts. It's all the rage. I earned it in the H-Blocks. The place is full of poets and writers. It's worse than the GPO (*points at Pearse/Declaration of Independence*) on Easter Monday.

AHERN: *Très bon* – I learned French there myself but it was a while back.

VICTOR: It also stands for Mother Fucking Animal.

AHERN: *(Beat).* Well it certainly becomes ya.

VICTOR: Which one?

AHERN: I'm sure you know the answer yourself. You ever think of doing a PhD?

VICTOR: I'm too busy. *(Beat).* I knew this guy once from Dundalk who said that P.H.D. were the three most important letters in the alphabet.

AHERN: Was this in one of your MFA workshops?

VICTOR: Not exactly – it was in a chop shop up in Ballymurphy. We had him in for a chat.

AHERN: What did you say?

VICTOR: I said, well no, the three most important letters in the alphabet are R.I.P. *(Beat).* Then I shot him. *(Beat).* In his head. *(Beat).* Through his E ... Y ... E.

AHERN: You're a laugh – that's a good yarn. (AHERN *gets up and goes to bar).*

VICTOR: I know. (*Beat*). True though.

AHERN: What's up anyway hey?

VICTOR: Pender wants to see you.

AHERN: Has that fart not retired yet?

VICTOR: No – not yet.

AHERN: (*Walks back*). I'll just finish this – no use wasting good drink.

VICTOR: Or blood.

AHERN: Jesus, you're a bit intense, aren't ya?

VICTOR: Someone has to be – that barman retard would have let a Para regiment in here.

AHERN: He's related to someone.

VICTOR: *(Shrugs).* He'll be related to that PhD RIP fucker if he doesn't watch out.

AHERN: *(Gestures towards the door).* Well, lead on McDuff. I took English Lit also.

VICTOR: Very droll. (*looks at* BARMAN *who cringes).* VICTOR *sits down, leans back feet on table, hands behind his head.* No, (*Beat*). Pender is outside, he's coming in.

AHERN: Ok. *(Beat).* Bring him on so. Can I buy you a drink? I have good credit here.

VICTOR: That's about the only place you have it.

AHERN: (*Indicating his glass to the* BARMAN). How do you mean? *(Beat).* What's this all about anyway?

VICTOR: *(to* BARMAN*):* PRO-FESS-SEWER where's my fucking tea? *(Beat).* Also get out to that black sierra and tell them it's sound as a pound to come in.

BARMAN: Sure, sure. Here's the tea. (BARMAN *hands him mug with teabag).*

VICTOR: (*Beat*). Have you no teapot? There is an art to making tea you know? Tea ceremonies are sacred in far away chink-land for example. No-one takes pride in their work anymore. Also get me a pack of Tayto.

BARMAN: (*Rushes back behind counter to get Tayto. Comes back. Puts on table*). They are extra.

VICTOR: Extra me hole. You are extra. You are extraneous. I am an essential cog of the Celtic Warrior killing machine. Jesus I have to shoot Brits and still pay for snacks. How do you like that?

BARMAN: It is in the bartending rulebook.

VICTOR: Fuck the rulebook.

BARMAN *wanders back to bar, forgets to go to the sierra.* VICTOR *clicks his fingers at the* BARMAN *who remembers it and rushes out.*

VICTOR: (*Calls after him*). Make sure to check the fucking street first. (*Beat*). Where we get that fucking eejit? He needs to be kneecapped (*Beat*) in the head.

AHERN: He's not that bad – guess who he's related to?

VICTOR: I could give a fuck.

AHERN: Suit yourself.

VICTOR *suddenly rushes over to the barcounter to raise the volume on the radio when he hears a song. Music: 'I Wanna Be Me' by* The Sex Pistols.

VICTOR: That's one of my favourite songs. I could dance to it all night. (VICTOR *does the pogo for 30 seconds with his arms held stiffly down by his sides in classical pogo fashion. He flicks his head at the highest point of each jump. Door bangs shut upstairs. The* BARMAN *comes back alone.* VICTOR *shouts over to him – each word below corresponding to the flick of his head at the climax of each jump*). DON'T ... LET ... ANY ... ONE ... ELSE ... IN ... SPECIAL ... LY ... ANY ... FUCK ... IN' ... JEH ... OVAH ... WIT ... NES ... SES.

PENDER *follows behind the* BARMAN. PENDER *shakes rain from his coat and watches* VICTOR *and looks over at* AHERN. *Then* PENDER *rushes over, turns down radio.*

PENDER: McGowan, what the holy fuck is going on here?

VICTOR: (*Fixing his hair*). Nothing – *relaxez vous.*

PENDER: Don't tell me to fuckin' relax – I'll fuckin' relax when I want to fuckin' relax. There were Brits everywhere – we had to drive away a few times.

VICTOR: I was just doing the pogo. It helps *moi* to relax.

AHERN *laughs.*

PENDER: You look like one of those Masai fuckers.

VICTOR: Well spotted Dr Pender-ston.

PENDER: What?

VICTOR: African history. Never mind.

PENDER: McGowan – I don't know what HQ sees in you but you're getting on my fucking nerves.

VICTOR: I have no nerves so naturally I don't know what you are feeling right now but I do respect that what you feel is genuine and that you must own your feelings and that ...

PENDER: Fuck up fucko!

VICTOR: Fuck up fucko – that's a good one. I will have to try that one out.

PENDER: I wish the good old days were back.

VICTOR: The good old IRA is it? – the good old days are a myth – they shot guys down dark alleys and kids off their bikes and guys in their beds and unarmed peelers and blindfolded RIC guys just like we do now. *Plus ca change* like.

AHERN: I thought that would appeal to you Victor?

PENDER: Ahern, keep out of this.

AHERN: *(Relaxed).* Jesus, Pender, you'd need to pogo for a decade to unwind. *(Beat).* Can I have a fag? (*He throws a crumpled up package on the floor).*

PENDER: No you can't – this is not a social club.

VICTOR: Well, it is actually – see on the bar counter there – 'The Padraic Pearse Lower Falls Social Club'.

PENDER: *(Exasperated).* You know fucking well what I mean.

AHERN: I only want one so I can pass the time while you two fight.

VICTOR: I don't call this fighting.

AHERN: Well whatever it is I'm dying for a fag.

PENDER: *(Shouting).* No fags fucker!

VICTOR: Wow – alliteration is your thing Pender – no fags fucker – fuck up fucko – I must remember all of them. I like them.

PENDER: Jesus, I'm too old for this.

VICTOR: Now you are talking.

PENDER: *(To* VICTOR). I told Doyle outside in the car to watch for Brits. Give him a code word will ya and get me a drink?

VICTOR: I don't fetch fucker (*Beat*) – wow it's contagious.

PENDER *looks at* VICTOR *– then indicates to the* BARMAN *he needs a drink.*

VICTOR: *(On Walkie-Talkie).* Doyle – wake up – the password is pogo.

DOYLE: *(Off stage).* You have to say 'come in' first and then follow it up with 'over' – over.

VICTOR: (*Annoyed).* What?

DOYLE: *(Off stage).* You have to say come in, to begin the interchange.

VICTOR: (*to* BARMAN *and* AHERN *and* PENDER *and audience*). Interchange! That's MFA talk where I come from.

DOYLE: (*Off stage*). You have to say over to …

VICTOR: I know I know – give it a rest – come in – over?

DOYLE: *(Off stage)* … complete the transmission over.

VICTOR: I'll fix your transmission – over.

DOYLE: *(Off stage).* That's better – over.

VICTOR: The fucking password is pogo – over.

DOYLE: *(Off stage).* What's the pogo – over?

VICTOR: Everyone must have been in the H-Blocks when this happened – over.

DOYLE: I don't copy – what's pogo over?

VICTOR: *(to the rhythm of 'Grease').*

Pogo's the word
the word –
it's got groove
it's got meaning
etc fuck me – over

DOYLE: *(Off stage).* What meaning – I don't copy – over.

VICTOR: Christ – pogo is the code fucking word – do you get it yet – you know in case any Brits or Jehovah Witnesses show up – do you fucking copy that – over.

DOYLE: *(Off stage).* Ok the dance – I got it now – like the Pistols and the Masai – I pogo – I mean I copy – over.

VICTOR: Yeah you're brilliant. (VICTOR *throws Walkie-Talkie on bartop then remembers he hasn't signed off. He goes back quickly and picks up Walkie-Talkie).* Over! (VICTOR *throws Walkie-Talkie back on bartop).*

PENDER: McGowan, are you and your boyfriend finished?

VICTOR: Yes sir! (*Does mock salute*). The interchange (*Sarcastically*) is over – over.

AHERN *laughs.*

PENDER: I don't know what anyone sees in you McGowan.

VICTOR: My mother used to say the same thing (*Beat*) but beauty is in the E.Y.E. of the beholder.

PENDER: What?

VICTOR: Never mind. Inside joke.

PENDER *stares at* VICTOR *and then moves his attention to* AHERN.

PENDER: *(From bar).* Sean – How have you been?

AHERN: Yeah, ok you know – staying out of trouble. The usual. *(Beat).* What's going on exactly? Do you have a new job for me? What's up with Mr MFA here?

PENDER: What's an MFA?

VICTOR: *(To* PENDER*).* Never mind that, let's stick to business.

PENDER: Don't tell me how to run things. We got on fine before you and we'll get on fine when you're gone.

VICTOR: I'm going nowhere.

AHERN: Victor is aiming for the top. He's a bright spark. He'll go far. Far. Far!

VICTOR: Unlike yourself – you're only going six feet and that's down. Down. Down!

AHERN: You're all talk.

VICTOR: We'll see.

PENDER: Excuse me *cailíní,* does anyone mind if I say something since I am the commanding officer here.

VICTOR: You are the ranking officer – it's not the same. Anyway – command away – no one is stopping ya.

PENDER: *(to* AHERN*).* I have got to ask you some serious questions.

AHERN: Ok – no problem. Shoot.

VICTOR *is strolling around. When* AHERN *says shoot,* VICTOR *quickly goes into gun stance aiming at* AHERN*'s head. Mimics firing. Mimics gun recoiling. Lips pursing to mimic shooting.* PENDER *looks up distracted.* AHERN *looks around.* VICTOR *has resumed strolling.*

PENDER: Well – you know about all these arms finds by the Brits?

VICTOR *sips his tea. He lifts the book that the barman had been reading.*

AHERN: Sure – there must be a leak somewhere.

VICTOR: You don't miss much.

PENDER: *(Beat).* Yeah there seems to be, ok.

AHERN: (*Stands up shouting).* You think it was me?

VICTOR: Jesus that's a good one – 'you think it was me?' – you should be on the stage.

PENDER: McGowan keep out of this. You're supposed to be just observing.

VICTOR: He's lying – I can feel it.

AHERN: Feel my dick why don't yeah?

VICTOR: Sorry, I never learned braille.

PENDER: McGowan – shut up.

VICTOR turns up volume dial on radio. Music: 'Suspect Device' by Stiff Little Fingers.

VICTOR: Clear the floor fuckers. Ah ha! Another one! (VICTOR *jumps into the centre of the floor. He does the pogo, pulls silver Colt and holds it down by his side as he dances. The light shines off the metal. He dances for 20–30 seconds).*

AHERN: (*Noticing the gun – gets nervous. Jumps up. Shouts above the noise).* Jesus – what's with the gun? (*Long beat. Shouts above the noise – keeps watching* VICTOR *and gun).* Look Pender what's this about?

PENDER *gets up, lowers volume.* VICTOR *stops dancing. Fixes his hair.*

VICTOR: You know what it's about. *(Beat).* Jesus that music is fucking deadly. I have to ask that DJ out. I hope it's a woman. I hope she has a great rack. (He *looks towards* PENDER). Of records.

PENDER: Keep that fucking radio turned down. The next time I'll shoot that fucking thing.

VICTOR: Let me shoot that funky thang – cool – it sounds like a soul number from Gladys Knight and the Pits or someone.

PENDER: *(leans against the bar facing away from* VICTOR *and* AHERN *and customers. Long beat, 15–30 secs*). It's the PIPS.

VICTOR: What?

PENDER: It's Gladys Knight and the fucking PIPS – (*angry)* it's the PIPS not the Pits.

VICTOR: I thought you hated Black culture.

PENDER: Jesus – not as much as I hate you.

VICTOR *and* PENDER *stare at one another. Long beat.* VICTOR *smiles. Gestures to* PENDER *to proceed with interrogation.*

PENDER: *(Focuses back on* AHERN). Ok Sean. Were you away?

AHERN: Yeah I was down in the south for a break.

VICTOR *strolls around the bar out of* AHERN*'s line of vision.*

PENDER: You're supposed to tell us.

AHERN: I thought it was ok.

PENDER: It's not ok if you don't tell us.

AHERN: Ok – I'll know next time

VICTOR: What next time?

AHERN: What?

PENDER: McGowan shut up. (*Beat*). It looked suspicious.

AHERN: Why?

PENDER: You go without saying and as soon as you go the Brits raid a safe house.

AHERN: It was just a coincidence.

PENDER: Who'd you meet down there?

AHERN: I stayed with … I met no one – it was just a break.

PENDER: You meet anyone you shouldn't have down there?

AHERN: No I said.

PENDER: We have a contact inside the RUC.

AHERN: Good good. *(Beat).* Who is it?

VICTOR: You sure are inquisitive? Why you want to know?

AHERN: No reason.

VICTOR: *(Disdainfully).* Yeah – right.

AHERN: Look lads there must be some mistake.

VICTOR: Save your breath. You'll need it soon.

PENDER: So Sean anyway this informant says we have a high-level tout.

AHERN: It's not me. (*Beat*). And how am I supposed to be tied into all this?

PENDER: He said this guy was high up, from Divis and had gunshot wounds in the back.

AHERN: Well I'm not from Divis and I have bullet wounds but so does half of Belfast.

PENDER: Yeah I know it's a bit vague but Victor here thought it was you for some reason. We tested you. We told no one else about the arms dump in Ballymurphy. It was raided a few days later.

AHERN: Jesus is that all – that's bullshit – anyone could have know about that. It could be just coincidence. You had me worried there for a minute.

VICTOR: *(From behind, bends down close to* AHERN*'s ear and says quietly).* And why is that?

AHERN is *startled.* VICTOR *hits him with gun to back of head.* AHERN *falls to the ground on hands and knees. He moans – holds his head.* VICTOR *pulls* AHERN *up and then sticks his gun between* AHERN*'s shoulder blades.*

VICTOR: Was your wee conscience bothering you? (VICTOR *frisks him thoroughly).* He's clean. Sorta. *(Wipes hands together as if to remove germs*).

PENDER: What the fuck is going on?

VICTOR: Jesus what's the problem? I'm getting bored – I thought he's supposed to be a big brave IRA warrior. (VICTOR *pushes* AHERN *away, who leans at the barcounter for support and checks his head for injury*).

AHERN: I did more for the cause than this little MFA faggot will ever do.

VICTOR *quickly pulls* AHERN's *left arm out straight, puts it on the barcounter and brings the gun down in short violent blows on his hand.* AHERN *screams and tries to resist.* VICTOR *bangs his head off the barcounter and* AHERN *falls back onto the floor).*

PENDER: McGowan! Keep the fuck out of this. How do you expect him to answer if he is semi-comatose?

VICTOR: Sorry to interrupt but that was personal.

PENDER: *(He furiously pulls his pistol and points it at* VICTOR). McGowan! (*He keeps the gun levelled at* VICTOR *who stares back and then* PENDER *slowly lowers his gun).*

VICTOR: If you ever point that gun at me again you better fucking use it.

AHERN: My fucking face.

VICTOR: It's not lethal, it just looks dramatic.

PENDER: Any chance we can finish this before the fucking Brits leave Ireland?

VICTOR: *(Looking at* AHERN. *Sarcastically).* Lead on McDuff.

PENDER: Who's McDuff?

VICTOR: Ask Ahern.

PENDER: Ahern – who is this McDuff guy?

VICTOR: (*Throws eyes to heaven. Exasperated).* He is fucking no one. The Scottish play thing.

PENDER: Rangers?

VICTOR: Jesus. Not football. The Bard of Fucken Avon. To Be or Not To Be Dead, Sonnet-land. (*Exasperated*).

PENDER: You fucking lost me!

VICTOR: (*Sarcastic*). Hard to believe! All hands lost. The captain goes down with his ship like the fucking Titanic.

PENDER: The Titanic is it? Don't start. It was built in Belfast but it was fine when it left here!

VICTOR: (*Exasperated*). The Titanic is like the IRA – air tight compartments allegedly. Never mind the fuck. Come on let's go. Chop chop!

BARMAN: (*Suddenly nervously speaking out of turn*). I ... I ... am dying for some Chinese. (*Everyone looks over.* BARMAN *puts up hands as if in surrender).* I am only saying.

VICTOR: Yeah?

BARMAN: Chew main.

VICTOR: Chow mein. I bet you order using numbers on the take out menu.

BARMAN: I also like ...

PENDER: Shut the fuck up will ya? – give me patience. (*Goes to bar, gets drink*). You have a fucking tapeworm Jimmy. (PENDER *turns towards* AHERN). Christ. Where was I? Ok – it looks pretty bad Sean. No one knew anything about that arms dump except you. There is no other reasonable explanation.

AHERN: Look lads this is fucked up – I hate touts – if I was one I would kill myself and not wait for you to do it.

PENDER: It looks bad.

AHERN: I killed all around me in the early days. What about those three paratroopers in Crossmaglen? People still talk about it.

PENDER: I know – but the facts are the facts.

AHERN: Fuck the facts. I don't care. It wasn't me. It isn't me. It never would be me.

PENDER: I don't know.

AHERN: It's not me. (*Long beat – 15 secs*).

PENDER (*To* VICTOR): I don't think it's him.

VICTOR: (*Shrugs*). Maybe.

AHERN: My fingers are broke.

VICTOR: – en Boo Hoo (*fists up to eyes as if child crying*) – it won't kill you – something else might though.

PENDER *looks around distracted.* VICTOR *goes to hold-all and takes out a lump hammer. A box of Barry's Tea falls out while he is rummaging in bag.*

VICTOR: Lump hammer time Ahern. That almost rhymes.

AHERN *moves away from the bar petrified holding his damaged hand. Walkie-Talkie crackles. Everyone jumps except* VICTOR *who throws the lump hammer aside.*

DOYLE: *(Off stage).* Come in – pogo – over.

VICTOR: *(Picking up Walkie-Talkie).* Yeah pogo – what's up?

DOYLE: *(Off stage).* You have to say over.

VICTOR: Over.

DOYLE: *(Off stage).* You have to say the full sentence followed by over – over.

VICTOR: What the fuck's up over – how's that – over.

DOYLE: *(Off stage).* You should only have one adverbial 'ov.er' in the interchange – over.

VICTOR: Adverbial me hole. How is this – fuck you – over.

DOYLE: *(Off stage).* Much better. The integrity of the exchange is safe. (VICTOR *mimics shooting the Walkie-Talkie).* Brit patrol – but it looks routine – over.

VICTOR: Ok – over.

PENDER *points gun towards the door.* BARMAN *anxiously moves around watching door. Beat.*

DOYLE: *(Off stage).* Ok first column gone past – looks grand – second column approaching – over.

PENDER, VICTOR, AHERN *and* BARMAN *wait in silence, looking expectantly. Then* AHERN *starts screaming.*

AHERN: Help! Help!

VICTOR *walks toward* AHERN *and hits him across the head with the Walkie-Talkie. Then punches him in the face as he tries to stand up.*

PENDER: Jesus!

VICTOR: Fuck, I knew it was him.

DOYLE: *(Off stage).* Keep it down in there.

VICTOR: You forgot to say over – over.

DOYLE: (*Off stage*). Give over – did I? Over.

VICTOR: You did – over.

DOYLE: *(Off stage).* I could have sworn I did say over though – over.

VICTOR: Well you did that time – over.

DOYLE: *(Off stage).* That's good – over.

VICTOR: I'm glad that's over – over.

VICTOR *throws the Walkie-Talkie on the bar counter.*

VICTOR: Ok, Ahern you know the drill – Get your clothes off – Down to your underwear – I hope they are clean – I have a touch of OCD – You know what I mean? – We haven't got all day. Especially you.

AHERN: Look lads you got this all wrong.

VICTOR: No fuckin' way. You yelled out to those Brits. (*Beat*). You wouldn't do that in a fit if you were innocent. (*Beat*). Take those trousers off or I'll cut them off. (VICTOR *shows knife in scabbard strapped onto his calf.* AHERN *reluctantly undresses one item at a time*). The pasty white Irish leg thing is downright unappealing. (VICTOR *picks up* AHERN*'s trousers which he had thrown at* VICTOR*'s feet.* VICTOR *imitating GAA commentator kicks the trousers across the stage*). In the dying moments of the game, the right back for Down scores the winning point. (VICTOR *does hands held aloft victory stance).*

AHERN: Look lads – I told them fuck all – it's all minor stuff – I never told them about the arms' dumps – I couldn't go back to the H-Blocks again – I'm a fucking hero in the IRA – No one will believe you.

VICTOR: People will believe what I tell them.

PENDER: This is not the proper procedure.

VICTOR: You being an IRA commander is not proper procedure as far as I'm concerned.

PENDER: HQ will hear about this.

VICTOR: I am HQ. They sent me to fix this mess.

AHERN: Please.

PENDER: What mess?

VICTOR: *(Pointing at* AHERN*).* This mess for instance. *(Beat*). You're a bit of a mess as well.

PENDER: What's that supposed to mean?

VICTOR: You run the most inactive Active Service Unit in all Belfast. You have guys disappearing down south on holidays. (*Grimaces*). You stock Walker's Crisps. You have fuckers like Ahern here vomiting their guts out to the Brits.

AHERN: Please. Pender?

VICTOR: Shut up Ahern. And YOU (*to Pender*) are wearing the worse suit I ever saw.

PENDER: *(Drinking the whiskey).* Fuck you McGowan.

VICTOR: And you're an alcoholic – you're a major liability.

PENDER: There is no way HQ will put up with this.

VICTOR: That's where you are wrong – HQ wants MFAs – HQ wants no fat – HQ wants results – HQ wants dead Brits – HQ wants action – I am action.

PENDER: I don't believe any of this.

VICTOR: Ok Ahern it's time.

AHERN: Jesus lads I don't believe this. (*Beat*). Please. (*Kneels up, raises his hands supplication wise with one hand distorted by the beating).* Are you happy now? Is that good enough for you?

VICTOR: (*Disgusted looking – looks away – is annoyed proceedings are delayed*). It's not good enough for me.

AHERN: Going back inside would have killed me.

VICTOR: Not like this is going to.

PENDER: Look the regulations say we have to have a court martial.

VICTOR: Fuck the regulations. The regulations say we have to win the war.

PENDER: I'm in charge here.

VICTOR: Barely. (VICTOR *picks up the lump hammer. He tests the weight).*

PENDER: Maybe we could ... do something.

VICTOR: We are. We are going to DO him.

PENDER: Maybe he can give us something. In exchange.

VICTOR *rushes towards* AHERN *who is kneeling at the table.* AHERN *cries out and cover his face.* VICTOR *smashes the Walker's Crisps on the table. Crisps go flying.*

VICTOR: Those crisps are an abomination sayeth the Lord. Penny Catechism. Graphic Novel edition.

PENDER: Fuck!

VICTOR: They were doing my head in. Them crisps.

PENDER: You are doing my head in.

VICTOR *roughly pushes* PENDER *out of the way.*

AHERN: Please. (*Shuffles around on knees following* VICTOR's *pacing).*

VICTOR: (*Sings opening lines from 'Please Release Let Me Go' by* Englebert Humperdinck). Please release me, let me go ... for I don't love you anymore. VICTOR *clicks fingers at* BARMAN *and points at radio to turn up the volume. MUSIC: 'Pull up to the Bumper Baby' by* Grace Jones. VICTOR *dances slowly toward* AHERN *from the back (freeform disco/house), dances towards hold-all, pulls out black hood, still holding gun in his hand.* VICTOR *dances in sync with the music. It is a sacrificial dance.*

AHERN: *(keeps pleading quietly – rocking himself as if a child comforting himself).* Please please!

MUSIC: 'How Soon is Now' by The Smiths. *When music starts* VICTOR *quickly pulls black hood over* AHERN*'s head, steps back and fires a shot.* AHERN *topples over.* VICTOR *leans in and fires* *a second shot.* AHERN*'s body spams slightly. Beat.* VICTOR *leans down again, fires a third shot. Blood flows from under the hood. The* BARMAN *looks over, shocked.* PENDER *stares from* AHERN *to* VICTOR *and back.* VICTOR *raises gun in the air as the music continues. Closes his eyes. Swaying still.*

PENDER: *(Rushes to bar, turns down radio).* McGowan – what the fuck is wrong with you – we didn't even start the court martial.

VICTOR: (*moves towards* PENDER *who retreats). Tempis fugit.* That's Latin. Who cares, he confessed didn't he? (VICTOR *keeps advancing.* PENDER *keeps retreating to bar counter and stops when he can't go any further.* VICTOR *leans into him.* PENDER *leans back).* We didn't even have to use the old burnt cigarette on the dick trick. Ah ha – that rhymes!

PENDER: You're out of control.

VICTOR: I'm more in control than you. You're shaking.

PENDER: *(Retreats back to table and sits down*). I'm reporting you as soon as we get back.

VICTOR: That sounds like tout talk. (*Beat*). Anyway back fucking where. It is a 360 degree front. There is only the front line. That is here.

PENDER: I'm reporting you for insubordination, for gross violation of court martial regulations, for ... for ... for abuse of barmen and ... and ... and dancing while on duty.

VICTOR: Take it easy before you induce a fucken aneurism.

PENDER: I'm reporting you. I don't care – this is no way to run an army. There is protocol you know – I am sick and tir ...

VICTOR *fires one shot at* PENDER *in the chest mid sentence who struggles to stay upright. Blood bursts from his chest. Blood comes out his mouth.*

VICTOR: 'Sick and Tired' – I hate clichés. They are a scourge of MFA programs.

VICTOR *leans against the bar, watches unconcerned. He waves goodbye at* PENDER *who falls face down on the table. He puts* PENDER*'s handgun in his belt.* VICTOR *blows out his breath as if the whole situation is a minor inconvenience.* BARMAN *still in shock behind bar watches and unsteadily grabs Luger from behind the counter and fumbles it. He nervously levels it at* VICTOR*'s back.*

BARMAN: Ah – hold it!

VICTOR: (*Unperturbed, slowly looks around and sees the* BARMAN *pointing the Luger at him, with hand tremors*). What's YOUR problem? Jesus did I miss something. Is it about not paying for the Tayto? You are very strict barkeep-rulebook wise.

BARMAN: (*Agitated*). That's my uncle.

VICTOR: Which one?

BARMAN: (*Faltering*). Ah, ah ... Pender.

VICTOR: Well he had it coming – he's old and a liability – plus he was doing my head in. (*Beat*). You know what that means! Just put the gun down – no harm done. (*Beat*). Yet.

BARMAN: But he's my FUCKING uncle.

VICTOR: Ex.

BARMAN: What?

VICTOR: Ex fucking uncle.

BARMAN: Ok, ok.

VICTOR: You ever see that TV show *The Man From U.N.C.L.E.?*

BARMAN: (*Nervously and incredulously*). Ah ... yeah I think so.

VICTOR: My mother loved that guy with the blond hair Illya Kuryakin. She would stop hitting us when it was on. Same with *The Fugitive*. He was always able to talk himself out of trouble, Kuryakin I mean. His middle initial was N. For Nickovetch. I have a thing about middle names. (*Beat*). He's not worth dying over. Just put the gun down.

BARMAN *looks flustered.*

VICTOR: (*Takes the Luger from the* BARMAN*'s hand*). This is a Luger I see. Great German precision engineering. That must be one of the ones they sent over to us in the good old days.

BARMAN: It was my grandfather's – it works – I tried it.

VICTOR: I'm sure it does work. Those Lugers never give any trouble. (*Beat*). Unlike yourself.

BARMAN: What?

VICTOR: Nothing. It's ok, I'm just joking. (*Pinches* BARMAN*'s cheeks playfully like with a baby*). Always so serious. (*Turns solemn*). It is ok. I know how it is with the old gene pool loyalty thing.

BARMAN: He's my fucking uncle. I feel I should do something.

VICTOR: Have a drink. (VICTOR *pours drink for him. He holds back drink momentarily)*. Are you legal age? Joke. (*Hands him drink*). It is memorial service Irish style.

BARMAN: (*Still holding gun but not raised. He drinks it*). It's not right.

VICTOR: *(Into Walkie-Talkie).* The pogo has landed – over.

DOYLE: *(Off stage).* What – over?

VICTOR: Nothing – it's just a little pun – over.

DOYLE: *(Off stage).* Gun – over?

VICTOR: No, pun – fuck, forget it. Pender won't be going back with us – over.

DOYLE: *(Off stage).* Jesus – what happened – over?

VICTOR: I'll tell you later – over.

DOYLE: *(Off stage).* Ok – what about Ahern – over?

VICTOR: (*Stands on* AHERN*'s broken hand*). No – he's over too. Drive round to the back door – over.

DOYLE: *(Off stage)*. Right, back – over.

VICTOR: (*On Walkie-Talkie*). That little white lie about the Brit patrol worked – over. (*He looks over at* BARMAN *who is sitting beside* PENDER *checking his chest wound*). Have you room for one more – over? (BARMAN *looks up startled.* VICTOR *pulls out his pistol. He levels the gun at the* BARMAN *as he starts the pogo to 'Should I Stay or Should I Go' by* The Clash).

THE END

INTERVAL MUSIC (*Provisional*)

Interval music between *Dancing at Lunacy* and *The Long Wet Grass* (depending on length)

'Teenage Kicks' by The Undertones

'Black is Black' by Los Bravos

Did You No Wrong, The Sex Pistols

II

The Long Wet Grass

Characters:

VICTOR: Head of IRA Internal Security, male (late 20s/early 30s)

WOMAN: VICTOR's Childhood Friend (late 20s/early 30s)

Setting: Callow Lake, Foxford, County Mayo. 14 August 1985, pre-dawn.

Curtain up.

MUSIC: *'Broken English' by* Marianne Faithfull.

Car sitting far stage left. Hazard lights on. Rest of stage in darkness. Music is lowered (by VICTOR *unseen), but not switched off. Low hum from engine.* VICTOR *steps out, slowly and deliberately. Looks out towards audience. Looks around. Cautious. Goes to trunk. Opens it. He helps a* WOMAN *out. She is stiff. She staggers a little – he steadies her – it takes her a while to straighten up. He unties the gag from her mouth.*

WOMAN: Wow – I am crippled.

VICTOR: I know. (*Beat*). Sorry.

WOMAN: My legs are shaking like a newborn calf's.

VICTOR: It will pass. (*Beat. Slowly*). All things pass.

WOMAN: Not everything. Not this. (*Beat*). How is this going to ever pass Victor can you tell me?

VICTOR: It will pass eventually. I just know.

WOMAN: You know nothing Victor.

VICTOR: How do you mean?

WOMAN: Never mind. I haven't got two years. How long was I in there anyway? It feels like forever.

VICTOR: Belfast to here – about 3 hours.

WOMAN: It was dark in there. It's even darker here. It is real country, deep black darkness.

VICTOR It's dark all over Ireland now.

WOMAN: That sounds like the snow falling passage in 'The Dead' – 'it covered all of Ireland – the living and the dead', Joyce.

VICTOR: I never went to college – I couldn't tell you.

WOMAN: Didn't you get an MFA?

VICTOR: That is not a real degree.

WOMAN: Well I am telling you. Joyce's wife Nora Barnacle was from your hometown Galway you know?

VICTOR: I knew that alright. Miss Galway 1909. It's the only thing Galway is famous for, except the Rahoon Flats, Druid, *The Quiet Man* and Lord Haw Haw?

WOMAN: Who?

VICTOR: You know 'jar-many calling jar-many calling' – during World War *a dó*. He went to the Jes school. Some guy broke his nose in the schoolyard. Hence the drawl.

WOMAN: How so uninteresting. (*Beat*). Did you know Nora Barnacle's boyfriend waited for her all night in the rain and then died of consumption?

VICTOR: Galway's middle name is rain. I like the rain. It cleans ...

WOMAN: (*Ignoring him and fast paced*). Anyway then Joyce – not your Nazi Joyce fucker – was consumed by Nora Barnacle. By her light. By her carnality. By her Galway *akkcent*. He had to carve up the English language instead of her dead boyfriend, even though he was long dead and lying in Rahoon cemetery high above the city. Jealousy was Joyce's middle name.

VICTOR: I walked past her house everyday going to school. I had a thing about her myself.

WOMAN: You have a thing about women that are not available. (*Gestures with arm)*. For example Nora Barnacle.

VICTOR: She is dead sure.

WOMAN: Yes – she's fucken perfect for you so! Your dead fucken gorgeous Galway girl. (WOMAN *sings lines of 'Galway Girl'*. VICTOR *looks around him till she stops)*.

'We were halfway there when the rain came down
Of a day -I-ay-I-ay
And she asked me up to her flat downtown
Of a fine soft day -I-ay-I-ay
And I ask you, friend, what's a fella to do
'Cause her hair was black and her eyes were blue

So I took her hand and I gave her a twirl
And I lost my heart to a Galway girl'.
[*'Galway Girl' by* Steve Earle].
Can I have a drink of water – I am parched.

VICTOR *takes bottle he has in his jacket pocket and hands it to her.*

WOMAN: You are always prepared – like the boy scouts!

VICTOR: I was never in them.

WOMAN: I know – I remember. The only kid in Mervue who wasn't. You were never an altar boy either. You were public enemy number one even back then!

VICTOR: The priest didn't like me. He said to my mother – that youngster has a dark cloud hanging heavy and low over him. He is a bit off. Take him off home with you.

WOMAN: Where's that guy now?

VICTOR: (*Points at himself, surprised by her question*). He is here.

WOMAN: Not you – what an egomaniac – I mean the fucken priest.

VICTOR: Oh he's away. In a dark place.

WOMAN: What?

VICTOR: Nothing. I am rambling. I am a bit nervous.

WOMAN: You are nervous! That's a fucken laugh. What about me?

VICTOR: I know. You are right. I am sorry you know …

WOMAN: (*Interrupting. She looks up).* I can see the stars. I feel close to heaven. The sky is beautiful.

VICTOR: (*Quietly*). You are beautiful yourself.

WOMAN: (*Does not hear him/ignores him*). The air smells so good here.

VICTOR: Yes – it is a very healthy location that way.

WOMAN: This place seems familiar.

VICTOR: It is.

WOMAN: *(Listens intently and stares into the distance far stage right, hears waves and can make out the bent black shadow of trees in the distance).* Is it near Callow Lake?

VICTOR: Yes.

WOMAN: Wow it's a long time since I've been back.

VICTOR: I know.

WOMAN: How do you know?

VICTOR: It's my job.

WOMAN: You are a true professional

VICTOR: Mostly. I try. I ...

WOMAN: *(Forced cheerfulness).* I remember we used to all dive off the rocks there in the summer before the death harmony of Belfast seduced you. You always said 'Banzai!' when you jumped. We never knew what that was.

VICTOR: It was in the *Victor* every week – you know Jap charges in Iwo Jima? Ma bought it every Friday in Holland's in Eyre Square. D.C. Thomson & Co. Ltd. was on the mast ...

WOMAN: *(Ignores him).* Those Callow Lake boys tried to kiss me in the long late light of those summer evenings.

VICTOR: I know.

WOMAN: Not you though!

VICTOR: Yeah – I mean no – I know.

WOMAN: You were as odd as two left feet.

VICTOR: I have found my feet now anyway.

WOMAN: We know – we know! Number one bad boy now.

VICTOR: Some people blossom late.

WOMAN: I would not call this here (*points around her*) fucken blossoming.

VICTOR: It depends. I suppose.

WOMAN: Not really. (*Long beat*). I am so afraid Victor.

VICTOR: I know.

WOMAN: (*Forced cheerfulness*). Do you remember that white Volkswagen Beetle you and Seán used to drive?

VICTOR: Sure. Yeah.

WOMAN: Do you remember that night coming from Killaser after the dance when we crashed on the slick wet road – I was scared.

VICTOR: I remember.

WOMAN: That girl Nadine in the back seat smashed into you – I remember the sound of heads clashing made me sick – you were bleeding all over the living and the near dead.

VICTOR: Her teeth cut my eyebrow wide open – it hurts still on cold nights.

WOMAN: You are such a romantic!

VICTOR: It has been said.

WOMAN: By fucken who? No one that's who. That's a pure lie.

VICTOR: Ok. (*Beat*). Ok – I know.

WOMAN: What happened to her?

VICTOR: Nothing. She went to England. She is in Dagenham. She married a Brit.

WOMAN: Wow that's death sentence right there.

VICTOR: Not really.

WOMAN: Since when?

VICTOR: Since always – he is a civilian Brit not a Brit Brit – so she is not a legitimate target.

WOMAN: Unlike me apparently. I liked her so I did.

VICTOR: I liked her myself.

WOMAN: You preferred me though.

VICTOR: Maybe.

WOMAN: You had a thing about me.

VICTOR: (*Slightly annoyed*). Maybe.

WOMAN: Is that why you never touched her?

VICTOR: *(Staring into the far away silhouettes of the black tress surrounding Callow Lake).* Maybe.

WOMAN: I wouldn't have minded if you did. Touch her you know?

VICTOR: *(Annoyed)*. Great! Good to know!

WOMAN: Good to know is it? Is that your answer – Jesus can't you say anything real?

VICTOR: (*Angry).* This is fucken real – here – now – this time – this black night – this Mayo river field – the promise of rain – Callow Lake – wind-break trees – this fucking car engine's hum – the radio playing low and longing – this gun. (*He pulls gun from belt*).

WOMAN: Jesus Victor – don't be killing me and you so angry – it is bad enough already – please please!

VICTOR: Fuck. (*He walks away).*

WOMAN *puts hands to her eyes, but doesn't cry. Can see her rib cage moving, ie silent sobs.* VICTOR *looks away again.* WOMAN *takes down hands. Looks at hands.*

WOMAN: I just remembered old Mrs Lawless examining my hands on the way back from the well – she stopped me on the road, put my palms face up, traced out the fresh creases made by the metal handles of the bucket that we used to fetch the water. 'Child you know you have townie hands. You are not made to be carrying well water. Go home with you now'.

VICTOR: She said the same to me as well. And me a boy!

WOMAN: She just had cataracts – it wasn't personal. Jesus. You had long shiny blue-black hair like an Indian so it was an easy mistake. Thinking you were a girl. I mean.

VICTOR: Maybe.

WOMAN: I never went back the road after that. She was scary. Her face was pitted with dust smuts embedded under her skin.

VICTOR: I did. I had to prove she was wrong.

WOMAN: You were always trying to prove something.

VICTOR: Maybe.

WOMAN: No one thought you had to prove anything. It was only you. It was in your head. The proving thing. The fucken Victor rulebook bollocks.

VICTOR: I had to prove it to myself anyway. If no one else.

WOMAN: No one else is right. You can sing that. What is this fucken proving? (WOMAN *spreads out her hands – turns all around).*

VICTOR: I am not sure.

WOMAN: You can prove something Victor NOW. And it will last forever.

VICTOR: Nothing lasts forever.

WOMAN: This can last forever Victor.

VICTOR: How? What?

WOMAN: You letting me go Victor. I will leave Ireland. I won't tell anyone. I will be far gone from Belfast and you.

VICTOR: It's too far gone now!

WOMAN: Please Victor. You loved me once back then, didn't you?

VICTOR: It's too far off now. The love song of killing can't be undone.

WOMAN: The love song of killing can't be undone, is it? What the fuck does that mean Victor? You think you are Joyce do you? (*Beat*). You think I am Nora Barnacle. (*Sarcastically*). Your dead Galway girl. She never read his stuff. She thought he was full of shit. You are full of shit. It's never too far gone Victor. Please.

VICTOR: You have to get ready. You know the story.

WOMAN: Fuck you. Fuck the story. (*She tries to run.* VICTOR *holds her steady. She stops. She leans against him. She starts to cry quietly).*

VICTOR: The rain is coming – I can smell it on the wind.

WOMAN: Fuck you and your weather forecast.

VICTOR: I am not too sure what to be saying.

WOMAN: I remember it always raining here.

VICTOR: Yeah it was. We were wet half the summer. And burned red the other half.

WOMAN: It was tricky trying to row on the lake out in the open with hard raindrops hitting you and the wind driving down from Culneachtain.

VICTOR: I didn't mind. At least it was warm rain. I like rain. It cleans the dark pure pla ...

WOMAN: (*Ignoring him, hurriedly*). Boys tried to kiss me when it rained.

VICTOR: The rain hides a lot.

WOMAN: I always looked over at you. For you. You were always looking away.

VICTOR: I never look away anymore.

WOMAN: You are looking away now, aren't you?

VICTOR: No – watching the dark far tree-line. Sometime I see shapes that are not the trees.

WOMAN: No surprise really. Some boys hung themselves from those strong slender trees.

VICTOR: Yeah. I know.

WOMAN: Some boys went quietly under the still Callow Lake surface.

VICTOR: Yes. I know.

WOMAN: Some boys dove off the tall rocks and broke themselves asunder.

VICTOR: I know.

WOMAN: Boys scared of everything. Of girls. Of girls' pale places. Of girls' dark places. Boys like you Victor.

VICTOR: (*Annoyed*). I'm still here, amn't I?

WOMAN: Only 'cause you had to prove you were not like them even though you were the purest example of them. Now I wish you had been one of them boys Victor.

Floating out to the far sea or hanging limp and lonely from those elm trees. I would not be here now.

VICTOR: It would just be someone else.

WOMAN: No. Anyone else would let it slide. Would let me be gone. Let bygones be bygones. But no – big bad Victor has to prove it. The most haunted one of them all is here today to prove his love to the cause.

VICTOR: Maybe.

WOMAN: Victor please!

VICTOR: I can't.

WOMAN: I didn't mean anything by it.

VICTOR: I know.

WOMAN: I didn't mean it at all. It was a momentary lapse. It was minor. That poor boy Brit soldier was dying. His eyes were eating me up. I could not look away. He was crying for his mother. He crawled in from the hard concrete to the garden to be lying on something softer. Something living. Something porous. Something closer to nature. Closer to the earth. Closer to heaven. There was black-red blood flowing out of him. There was so much. It was as black as the night is here. I was thinking of his mother. The poor woman. And him. And him dying far, far, far from home in a West Belfast street. All he could see was the hills of Belfast, and the towers of Divis and my face. It was only a drink of water. I held his shaking hand so he could hold it. He was trying to tell me something. I bent down close so I could hear what he said. (*Beat*). He said 'I am so afraid'. Blood droplets were coming out of his mouth. His teeth were so white. I remembered that. It is funny the things you remember. He said …

VICTOR: (*Very agitated*). I know – I know! Jesus. (*Beat. More composed*). I know all that.

WOMAN: Is it so bad?

VICTOR: (*Bothered).* No. Not so bad. (*Beat*). But it's in the rules.

WOMAN: (*Frustrated).* Fuck the rules. (*Beat*). Victor please.

VICTOR: It can't be undone – the needle is in too deep.

WOMAN: What fucking needle – what are you talking about?

VICTOR: You know yourself.

WOMAN: No – I don't know – this is not Top of the Fucken Pops. Victor for me. For old times? Look at me Victor.

VICTOR *looks at her.*

VICTOR: There are no old times anymore – there is only Callow Lake and the dark and the swaying black shadows. And the rain soon coming off the bare black mountain.

WOMAN: There is us Victor.

VICTOR: There is no us.

WOMAN: There was. You just didn't know it.

VICTOR: There is no us.

WOMAN: Well at least there is me. There is life here and in me and in the wind and in the deep lake where black eels swam away from me and there is life in those trees that are bent crooked by the wind coming down off the mountains that I loved. And that loved me back. (*Cries quietly*). And I was a girl here once. I watched out for you walking the road. And the river fields. And you never looked over.

VICTOR: I never knew.

WOMAN: You never knew anything. You still don't. You're a disease Victor I fucken caught. You are pure stupid.

VICTOR: Jesus – I am supposed to be Mensa material!

WOMAN: That just proves it. You are the thickest genius I ever saw. *(Long beat, 10 seconds – composed now).* Look Victor. It's ok. I give up. I know the story. I am sorry. I know it's a hard thing. For you. For anyone.

VICTOR: It's hard all over.

WOMAN: Is it soon?

VICTOR: Soon enough.

WOMAN: Victor – don't tell me when exactly.

VICTOR: Ok.

WOMAN: I won't be lost out here (*gestures*) will I, in the long wet grass?

VICTOR: No – I will make sure.

WOMAN: Ok. Victor I am glad it's you though. I bet you could have given it to someone else.

VICTOR: I suppose.

WOMAN: You are probably trying to prove something – the fucken usual.

VICTOR: Sure.

WOMAN: I am brave overall though, amn't I Victor?

VICTOR: Yeah. You are. You were always. I saw it long ago. A long way off.

WOMAN: I didn't mean to cry.

VICTOR: Ah – it wasn't much.

WOMAN: I never usually beg.

VICTOR: I know. It wasn't much.

WOMAN: Victor you were always too much. You only had to ask.

VICTOR: You never said.

WOMAN: (*Resigned*). No. Not directly. (*Beat*). Will they find me quick, do you think?

VICTOR: -Ly. (*Beat*). Yes.

WOMAN: Do you promise?

VICTOR: Yes.

WOMAN: That's good anyway. I know you keep promises. It's in your fucken rule book.

VICTOR: I would anyway.

WOMAN: Can you hold me Victor?

VICTOR: Ahh – Jesus – I am not great at it really.

WOMAN: If you can't it's ok. No use changing the habit of a lifetime I suppose.

VICTOR: I will try so.

WOMAN: *(Leans in to him. He puts his arms around her hesitatingly. She cries quietly. She breaks contact after 30 seconds).* You promise I won't be lost out here in the long wet grass like Winnie Battle long ago. She waited there all night for someone.

VICTOR: Yes I know. For my mother.

WOMAN: My mother will be bad enough already.

VICTOR: You won't be lost. They will find you easy. I will tell them.

WOMAN: I am ok now Victor. Weariness was pulling me under anyway. It's as deep as Callow Lake's black pool places. The last six months have been terrible.

VICTOR: I know.

WOMAN: How long did you know?

VICTOR: Fairly soon. I tried to prove it was wrong. You were careless.

WOMAN: You could have lied.

VICTOR: I suppose.

WOMAN: Well we are together at last anyway – just you and me and the rain coming fast from Collneachtain. Your favourite. (*The* WOMAN *listens intently to a song from car radio).* I love that song Victor. (WOMAN *softly sings first line from 'And I Miss You' by* Everything But The Girl). 'And I miss you, like the desert misses rain …' You remember that song Victor?

VICTOR: Kinda.

WOMAN: I often hum it to myself. So strange to hear it now.

VICTOR: It's some disco shit isn't it?

WOMAN: No it's great – at the school hops in Killasser. Don't you remember?

VICTOR: I never went inside.

WOMAN: I remember – you sat on the wall outside like a fucken eejit. Everyone thought you were gay.

VICTOR: No!

WOMAN: I know Victor – fucken relax. (*Beat*). Can I turn it up?

VICTOR: Ok.

She walks to the car. Turns up volume. Music: on the car radio 'I Miss You' by Everything But The Girl.

WOMAN: Can I dance for a few minutes?

VICTOR: Ah – I suppose – ok – go ahead.

She sways to the music. She moves around. She approaches VICTOR. *She kisses him on the lips. She resumes dancing. She has her eyes closed, swaying to the beat.* VICTOR *lifts the gun – he follows her movements for 20 seconds. He is unsure. He lowers the gun. The* WOMAN *keeps dancing. After 5 seconds when it looks like he will let her be, he suddenly lifts the gun and shoots her in the head twice. She falls. A dog starts barking. Rooks noisily rise from the trees surrounding Callow Lake.*

VICTOR: (*puts his forearm against his eyes. The gun is still in his hand. After 10 seconds he fires 4 shots into the air saying in a rage with each shot).* Fuck – fuck – fuck – fuck. (VICTOR *stands still with arm raised up until all is quiet again – dogs stop barking, birds stop calling. He walks back to the car. Leaves the trunk open. He throws the gun into the car. He turns up the radio. He crouches down by the side of the car – shaken – both palms over his eyes. The song keeps playing).*

THE END

INTERVAL MUSIC

Interval music between *The Long Wet Grass* and *Boys Swam Before Me.*

An tAiseiri (The Resurrection) by Nóirín Ní Riain
Seacht Suailici na Maidhine by Nóirín Ní Riain
Ar nAthair (Our Father) by Nóirín Ní Riain

III

Boys Swam Before Me

Characters:

VICTOR: Head of IRA Internal Security, male (late 20s/early 30s)

MAY MCGOWAN: Victor's mother (60s)

Setting: Nursing House in County Galway. Night, 14 Aug 1986.

Curtain up.

Bedroom of Nursing Home in County Galway. Lights on. Lamp on bedside locker. Door facing corridor has glass panel. Woman in bed. Bedclothes disturbed. She lies in foetal position. One hand curled up clings to the raised bedguard. With other hand curled she rubs her eyes with her curled fist. VICTOR *comes in through window. Silver Colt in his hand. Drops to floor in military-like stance. He has heavy facial bruising on left side of face, black eye is partially shut. Looks around. Walks to door. Looks through small glass panel in door. Checks his face in wall mirror. Touches his face tentatively. Flinches in pain. He walks over to bed. He crouches down. Watches his mother. He tries to loosen her hand from the guardrail. She resists. He sits in chair, strokes her hair for a second. Quickly stops. She mutters and occasionally whimpers. Then she wakes up.*

MAY MCGOWAN: Paddy?

VICTOR: No Ma! It's just me. Victor.

MAY MCGOWAN: Paddy, is that you? You are the best brother ever.

VICTOR: Jesus – you don't take no for an answer very easily – Ma – it's me. Big bad Victor. (*Beat*). I thought I was supposed to be your favourite! It's the only advantage of being the newborn king. Son, I mean. (*Beat*). Whatever happened to imprinting I'd like to know?

MAY MCGOWAN: Whatever happened your eye? Come closer Paddy. (*Beat*). Jesus. That is atrocious. Have you been jumping off balconies again?

VICTOR: (*Startled*). What? Of course not. No, no – Brits did this. SAS fuckers you know yourself. Also I bruise easily. Veganism.

MAY MCGOWAN: (*Appalled*). You are a Jew now?

VICTOR: Veganism – not Judaism.

MAY MCGOWAN: That is nearly worse. Dietary deficiency.

Rickets. Smallpox, tape worms, jaund-ICE, thrush. Kuru.

VICTOR: (*In typical* VICTOR *mode, he gestures with hands*). Kuru you get from cannibalism! Hence veganism incompatibility. Jesus!

MAY MCGOWAN: Watch your fucking language young man.

VICTOR: (*Contrite*). Ok Ma sorry! *Mea culpa.*

MAY MCGOWAN: That's Latin.

VICTOR: Yeah I know.

MAY MCGOWAN: If you were sorry you wouldn't say it!

VICTOR: Your favourite expression.

MAY MCGOWAN: You should try Optrex for that eye.

VICTOR: Ok.

MAY MCGOWAN: Optrex is great. (*Beat*). Although it is patent pending.

VICTOR: (*In admiration*). The things you know.

MAY MCGOWAN: I do not know you. (*Beat*). I'm perished. It's freezing in here. Were you born in a stable?

VICTOR: If only! (VICTOR *stands up, pulls up her bedclothes).* You were always cold Ma. It's a real McGowan thing. I didn't get it. (*Beat).* But I got everything else though.

MAY MCGOWAN: Is that you Paddy? You're late again – How was school? – Make sure you do your homework. You have to go to college. I could never go myself. Even though I was first in the Leaving in County Mayo.

VICTOR: (*Mimics along with her*). 'Even though I was first in the Leaving in County Mayo'. (*Beat*). Sure Ma.

MAY MCGOWAN: Don't 'Sure Ma' me – you know your father will kill us all if you don't get to college.

VICTOR: Sure he killed us all multiple times over already. (*Beat*). You were pretty good at it yourself if memory serves me and it should since ...

MAY MCGOWAN: (*Agitated interrupting*). Will my Daddy come to see me soon?

VICTOR: Yes Ma.

MAY MCGOWAN: He won't forget me? He won't leave me lying lost here? (*Beat*). Will my Daddy come before long?

VICTOR: Sure Ma – he'll be in later. They have to drive up from Mayo.

MAY MCGOWAN: It's a fair trek.

VICTOR: You're right Ma.

MAY MCGOWAN: (*Singing in tuneless cracking voice).*

'Home to Mayo, home to Mayo –
someone is waiting for you I know
in the firelight her eyes will be bright –
and your heart's in the cottage in county Mayo'

VICTOR: (*Puts hands over ears*). Jesus Ma you are tone deaf.

MAY MCGOWAN: Don't take that tone with me sonny. (*Beat*). I can still put you on the rack. (*Beat*). I'll go back home to Mayo? To Callow Lake?

VICTOR: Of course Ma. Soon.

MAY MCGOWAN: I was happy there once.

VICTOR: I know. Everyone was apparently.

MAY MCGOWAN: Winnie Battle died there though.

VICTOR: (*Throwing eyes to heaven – heard it all before).* I know Ma.

MAY MCGOWAN: Winnie Battle died in the river field near Callow Lake. She was alone. The tall rushes hid her till morning time. The fat stems were full and heavy with rain but they did not bend over. In the warm Mayo night they swayed before her.

VICTOR: It's ok, Ma. Callow Lake hides a lot.

MAY MCGOWAN: She was my friend. She loved me. She waited for me. I never came.

VICTOR: Sure Ma I know. It's ok. You didn't know.

MAY *becomes agitated. She cries quietly.* VICTOR *hesitates, then strokes her forehead for a second only. Pulls his hand back.*

MAY MCGOWAN: I was over at Callow Lake. She waited long for me. I didn't know. (VICTOR *lies on floor to help ease his back pain).* Callow boys beautiful swam before me.

VICTOR: (*On floor*). You were like a fecken mermaid Ma.

MAY MCGOWAN: (*Shouts out suddenly – frightened*). Daddy – Daddy!

VICTOR: (*On floor*). It's ok Ma.

MAY MCGOWAN: I'm so afraid …

VICTOR: (*On floor*). It's ok Ma – it will pass – all things pass – I'll stay a while.

MAY MCGOWAN: Paddy – for Jesus' sake can you help me?

VICTOR: (*On floor*). Ma – it's me Victor.

MAY MCGOWAN: Victor who? I do not know any Victor. Only the comic. I bought it every Friday evening in Holland's on Eyre Square. (*Beat*). It had DC Thomson & Co. Limited on the masthead. I will remember that as long as I live. It just seems like yesteryear.

VICTOR: (*On floor*). Yesteryear – very Victorian I must say!

MAY MCGOWAN: (*Agitated*). I do not know any Victor I just said.

VICTOR: (*On floor. Sad*). Ok Ma. *Relaxez vous.*

MAY MCGOWAN: How can I relax? It is like the fucking Arctic in here. Where am I anyway? (*Looks around. Can't see* VICTOR*)*. I am hearing voices. Is Daddy here?

VICTOR: (*On floor*). No Ma – Daddy's not here yet. He is coming though soon.

MAY MCGOWAN: Daddy I'm so afraid. Daddy!

VICTOR: (*mimics back stroke on floor*). It's ok Ma.

MAY MCGOWAN: Boys swam before me. Boys jumped from the high black shadow rocks shouting out to me 'May McGowan look at me will ya?' – I swam deep – I would look up at the water above me and see their bodies distorted as they jumped and then landed. My long black hair floated behind me.

VICTOR: (*On floor*). Wow, a speech – you are full of surprises.

MAY MCGOWAN: Daddy didn't like those boys.

VICTOR: (*On floor*). Daddy was smart. (VICTOR *reaches wall and swivels slowly 180 degrees. Then pushes off from wall with legs – mimics again slow backstroke back towards the foot of the bed).*

MAY MCGOWAN: Daddy said I had slick black hair. Like a Cheyenne he said. I should be riding across the Indian plains of North Dakota.

VICTOR: North Mayo more like! (*He gets up and sits on chair).*

MAY MCGOWAN: I always wanted to be a Cheyenne after that.

VICTOR: I know Ma. Sure I got Indian outfits every year for Christmas. I was a nervous wreck on Christmas Day waiting to see. And hoping against hope. I was the only redskin in Mervue. I had to run for my life till the end of January from all the Jesse James and Wyatt Earps. No Irish. No dogs. No Blacks. No Injuns. At least the Indian eagle war feather you gave me was authentic!

MAY MCGOWAN: I wanted to race through long meadow grass and never look behind me again. Forever and never amen. (*Blesses herself).*

VICTOR: (*Thoughtfully).* I know what that's like.

MAY MCGOWAN: (*repeats the song*).
'Home to Mayo, home to Mayo
someone is waiting for you – I know –
in the firelight her eyes will be bright
and your heart's in the cottage in county Mayo'

VICTOR: (*Covering his ears).* It gets no better on heavy rotation.

MAY MCGOWAN: Where is your girl? She reminded me of me. She watched out for you. I never see her anymore.

VICTOR: (*Cautious*). What girl?

MAY MCGOWAN: Daddy! Daddy! I'm so afraid.

VICTOR: It's ok Ma.

MAY MCGOWAN: Boys called out to me loud and longing.

VICTOR: (*Embarrassed*). Long, you mean?

MAY MCGOWAN: Boys called out to me from the long drop rocks.

VICTOR: Wow – poetry! (VICTOR *fixes her pillow).* How come you picked Da when all those Callow boys did backward somersaults off the rocks to impress you?

MAY MCGOWAN: (*Smiling).* He said to me 'May McGowan you have black shiny hair like an Indian'.

VICTOR: Well you had to pick him so then.

MAY MCGOWAN: Daddy! Daddy! I want to go home to Callow Lake.

VICTOR: Jesus Ma keep it down. Do those nurses ever do night rounds? You could be dead and gone and they wouldn't know until they tried to wake you for breakfast. At least the place is spotless. You could eat your dinner off that floor. If you knew what a dinner was.

MAY MCGOWAN: Sometimes I see the River Moy pulling boys out to sea. Sometimes I see boys slide under the surface of Callow Lake. Sometimes Winnie Battle waits for me.

VICTOR: You are a laugh a minute!

MAY MCGOWAN: Sometimes Bernie cries. (*Beat*). Sometimes Victor cries.

VICTOR: (*Being smart*). Sometimes doves cry!

MAY MCGOWAN: Prince!

VICTOR: Impressive Ma!

MAY MCGOWAN: Sometimes I dream of my first baby. He had blue-black shiny hair. Like an Indian. Like me.

VICTOR: (*Puts hand through his hair proud*). Sure!

MAY MCGOWAN: I would have preferred a blondy though

like Illya Kuryakin for sample.

VICTOR: (*Disappointed*). I see, ok.

MAY MCGOWAN: Kuryakin was in *The Man from U.N.C.L.E.* He was the one-armed bandit in *The Fugitive* as well but he had black hair in that. And only one arm.

VICTOR: He was versatile I will say that about him.

MAY MCGOWAN: Another verse? Ok.

'Home to Mayo ...

VICTOR: (*Interrupts*). Tell me more about Victor.

MAY MCGOWAN: I hated him.

VICTOR: (*Startled*). What?

MAY MCGOWAN: He nearly died deep inside me. He nearly strangled himself with that bloody Richard Kimble chord thing you know? (*Beat*). He is killing ever since. (*Beat*). He never kills girls though.

VICTOR: (*Sad, knows it is true, except for once*). That is good anyway.

MAY MCGOWAN: He nearly killed me though.

VICTOR: How do you mean?

MAY MCGOWAN: He scared me. Inside he scarred me. (*Beat*). He was a lot of trouble.

VICTOR: Not really? Was he? I do not think he was ...

MAY MCGOWAN: Daddy! Daddy!

VICTOR: Jesus. Never mind. Very effective anti-interrogation technique. That runs in the family for sure. It's ok, Ma. Shhh. Try not to worry. It will pass.

MAY MCGOWAN: *(Appalled).* Mother of God – what happened to that eye – did you injure it jumping off the rocks?

VICTOR: *(Annoyed).* I might have if I knew you would remember me. (*Beat. Calmer*). No, no – an accident is all.

MAY MCGOWAN: Victor was an accident.

VICTOR: Jesus – this is a great visit so far. (*Beat*). Will I try Optrex? Even though it is patent pending.

MAY MCGOWAN: Patent pending is it? Is that supposed to be the Queen's English? (*Beat*). Is that some kind of code word? Are you trying to cod me? (*Beat*). Optrex is your only man. (*Beat*). You are a good boy Paddy.

VICTOR: Not really.

MAY MCGOWAN: (*Spotting gun*). Is that a Luger I see before me?

VICTOR: (*Startled, he takes it out*). No. No. A Colt. A 45. 1911. Officer issue. You are losing your touch in your old age.

MAY MCGOWAN: (*Laughing, puts hands up*). Don't shoot. I am innocent of all charges! You can let it slide! It was nothing much.

VICTOR: (*Unsettled*). Ok Ma – May I mean. (*Beat*). What was nothing much?

MAY MCGOWAN: You know.

VICTOR: Not really. What do you me …

MAY MCGOWAN: Paddy, *tá mé treachta.*

VICTOR: Ok, Ma … May.

MAY MCGOWAN: Ok Paddy (*Long beat*). Do you ever see wee Victor?

VICTOR: (*Hesitant*). Ah yeah – sometimes you know. He is up North.

MAY MCGOWAN: He is number one bad boy – he never comes to see me.

VICTOR: (*Hesitant*). Ahh now he does you know. He tries. I think.

MAY MCGOWAN: Did you hear the latest?

VICTOR: (*Exasperated*). No! Go on!

MAY MCGOWAN: He is Jewish now. He will go straight to hell. Where did I go wrong?

VICTOR: He is not Jewish May – he is still a Catholic. He is a vegan only. It is not so bad is it? He was nearly an altar boy. Remember?

MAY MCGOWAN: Father Leper didn't like him.

VICTOR: Father Leeper.

MAY MCGOWAN: He sent Victor away from the church.

VICTOR: (*Quietly*). I sent him away.

MAY MCGOWAN: I was mortified. The neighbours could not stop talking about it.

VICTOR: (*Exasperated, punches the air in frustration like boxer. Quietly*). Fuck the neighbours. (*Beat. Calms down gradually*).

MAY MCGOWAN: He was afraid of everything. Inside he was girl material. That is why his middle initial is M. (*Beat*). M stands (VICTOR *puts his hands over his ears*) for Mary. The Assumption into Heaven.

VICTOR: Jesus. Can't you give it a rest. You are doing my head in. That name murdered me. Don't you know anything? M is for mercy – you have none. Bad enough being a fucken Indian without being a squaw as well.

MAY MCGOWAN: (*Calmly*). You can't deny your heritage.

VICTOR: (*Exasperated*). I am not a fucking Indian. I am 100% Irish sure. I have no Geronimo blood. I burn in the sun after 5 seconds, *ipso facto* I am Irish.

MAY MCGOWAN: (*Calmly*). Geronimo was not a Cheyenne.

VICTOR: (*Exasperated*). You know well what I mean.

MAY MCGOWAN: Paddy, I would love to see Victor even if it was just the once. (*Beat*). He wasn't all bad. The kuru might have damaged him.

VICTOR: No. (*Beat*). It was you.

MAY MCGOWAN: I was a nurse you know? On Iwo Jima.

VICTOR: (*Exasperated*). It was Inisheer. (*Nods*). Ok. Ok. Sure. I know you were. I will let Victor know about the visit. He will be happy to hear that.

MAY MCGOWAN: Victor Kuryakin, I used to call him.

VICTOR: Yeah I remember.

MAY MCGOWAN: He was not in love with that name I can tell you.

VICTOR: (*Annoyed*). It was better than the fucking M for Mary thing!

MAY MCGOWAN: I am kind of rambling. (*Sings*).

'I'm a rambler, I'm a gambler
I'm a long way from home
And if you don't like me
Just leave me alone'
['*The Moonshiner' by* Delia Murphy]
Delia Murphy sang that. She was from Mayo.

VICTOR: (*Quietly*). Fuck Delia Murphy.

MAY MCGOWAN: I forget things. I mix things up. My head hurts.

VICTOR: You always suffered in silence.

MAY MCGOWAN: I can't keep my eyes open.

VICTOR: Good! Joke! It's alright. (*Beat*). It's alright. It's ok to sleep now. (*Jokingly*). Even though you escaped the war tribunals for that singing. And throwing Victor off the balcony.

MAY MCGOWAN: It was only the second floor.

VICTOR: Good job he was so supple so!

MAY MCGOWAN: Paddy don't forget to tell my boy Victor about the girl.

VICTOR: (*Troubled*). What girl?

MAY MCGOWAN: He was in love with that fecken girl but he didn't even know. He was dense that way. He needed Optrex for the brain that fella.

VICTOR: What girl?

MAY MCGOWAN: She waits for him. Winnie Battle waits for me.

VICTOR: Where does she wait?

MAY MCGOWAN: Near Callow Lake. She called over all the time. For him. I never told him.

VICTOR *looks stricken. Looks away.*

VICTOR: Why did you not tell me … him? Victor I mean.

MAY MCGOWAN: Tell who what? I am so tired.

VICTOR: You said something about Victor's girl – you know?

MAY MCGOWAN: Did Victor have a girl? That's news to the likes of me.

VICTOR: You were saying about …

MAY MCGOWAN: (*Pinches his cheeks*). Always so angry!

VICTOR: (*Agitated. Pulls hand away).* Give it a rest can't you? You are doing my head in. (*Beat*). No wonder I ran away from home.

MAY MCGOWAN: (*Agitated*). I am NOT at home. (*Annoyed*). Do you think I am fucking senile or what?

VICTOR: (*Exhausted. Placatory*). No. No. You are not.

MAY MCGOWAN: (*Agitated*). Of course I amn't. Don't you know the first thing about anything?

VICTOR: (*Bewildered*). Not really. I thought I knew everything but now ...

MAY MCGOWAN: Sometimes I wake up screaming. Sometimes I see black coelacanths devour me. They are eyeless. I have to pray to stop them swallowing me. (*She begins to pray in Irish).*

'Sé do bheatha, a Mhuire,
atá Lan de ghrásta,
Tá an Tiarna leat.
Is beannaithe thú idir mná,
Agus is beannaithe toradh do bhroinne; Íosa.
A Naomh-Mhuire,
a Mháthair Dé,
guigh orainn na peacaigh,
anois, agus ar uair ár mbáis.
Amen'.

VICTOR *gets up as she prays. Looks at her. Trying to figuring out what to do. He goes to the table and lets a tablet fall onto his hand from the bottle. He pours a glass of water. When his mother stops he stands beside the bed. He holds the glass in his hand.*

MAY MCGOWAN: Paddy – you are here at last.

VICTOR: Yes Ma ... May. Sorry it took so long.

MAY MCGOWAN: How is everyone in North Dakota?

VICTOR: I give up.

MAY MCGOWAN: Is Daddy with you?

VICTOR: (*Quietly*). He is not too far off now. Here's a glass of water. (*Beat*). Here is your tablet – they must have forgotten it.

MAY MCGOWAN: Ok Paddy. (MAY *sticks out tongue as if receiving communion.* VICTOR *puts the white tablet on her tongue. She closes her eyes).*

VICTOR: The body of Christ.

MAY MCGOWAN: Amen! (*She leans back.* VICTOR *strokes her brow*).

VICTOR: Did you hear the latest?

MAY MCGOWAN: What?

VICTOR: Victor converted back to Catholicism.

MAY MCGOWAN: *Deo gratias*. I have to tell Father Leper. So Victor can be an altar boy after all?

VICTOR: Yes. He will go straight to heaven!

MAY MCGOWAN: (*Long beat*). So tired. (*She looks into his eyes).* I am on no tablets Paddy.

VICTOR: (*Hesitant*). I know May. It's ok. (*Beat).* Daddy said it's ok.

MAY MCGOWAN: Sound as a pound. (*Beat*). I am sinking under the waves of Morpheus so I am! He was a Greaseball!

VICTOR: A Greek you mean.

MAY MCGOWAN: Paddy?

VICTOR: Yes?

MAY MCGOWAN: Never tell Victor about the girl. (*Beat*). It will kill him.

VICTOR: I know.

MAY MCGOWAN: Hums 'Home to Mayo' for a few seconds. (*Beat. Opens eyes).* I was a nurse on Iwo Jima. (*Beat*). There were Japs everywhere. I was in the *Victor*. They jabbered in Irish day and night. It did my head in. I had to pick it up fast but I am Mensa material. At night the island was as dark as a newly-minted Black Baby.

VICTOR: There were no Japs or Blacks on Inisheer.

MAY MCGOWAN: I saw babies blood-slide out and die before me. (*Beat).* I saw the celestial blue light leave them slowly. (*Beat*). In Callow Lake lithe white Irish boys died *très* lonely. (*Beat*). I saw Victor jumping off the balcony like a black eagle. (*Beat*). I laid out drowned fishermen on tables who were still dripping Atlantic water off their strong fingers. (*Beat*). I can hear the drips sometimes hitting the stone floor. It is funny the things you remember.

VICTOR: So I heard. I ... (*Stops suddenly when he realizes she is dead*).

MAY MCGOWAN *dies. He lets go of her arm and it drops on top of the bedspread.* VICTOR *closes her eyes. He blesses himself. He walks back to the bedside locker. He pulls out a model (plastic/metal) of an Indian brave on a galloping black horse, war bonnet trailing behind him, a lance poised to throw. He turns the main light off. Diffuse light from the corridor shines in. He places the model on the bedside locker. He places the bedside lamp so the image of the charging brave is projected onto the wall. He makes some minor adjustments until it is just right. He walks to the window. He looks around one last time studying everything so he won't forget any of it. He does a farewell gesture with his hand. Opens the window. Climbs out.*

THE END

POST SHOW MUSIC (*Provisional*)
'Gimme Shelter' by The Rolling Stones
'The Galway Girl' by Steve Earle
'The Power of Love' by Frankie Goes to Hollywood
'Mandika' by Sinéad O'Connor

Steven Simring

AFTERWORD

The McGowan Trilogy is a study in psychopathy. Victor is a true psychopathic killer, which is a rarity in literature. Sure, there are lots of mass slayers and serial murderers and psychotic butchers. But they are different. Mass slayers have a grudge to settle; serial murderers are sexually preoccupied; and psychotic killers are out of contact with reality. Even genocidal monsters usually have a political point to make.

Not so with Victor McGowan. Victor is supposedly advancing the cause of the Irish Republican Army, where he has some kind of enforcer or leadership position. Surely, British spies are a major problem and have to be dealt with quickly, even summarily. Whacking double agents is a piece of unpleasant, but necessary business. And that is what Victor claims he does. But how does he decide who is a spy? And why does he enjoy it so much?

Victor is not psychotic and he is not dumb. He is actually quite smart and his reality testing is perfectly intact. He is Gaelic, but he speaks English like a poet. He is sort of a young Irish Hannibal Lecter, a psychopathic killer who speaks so beautifully, you can cry. The alliterations roll off his tongue: 'the three most important letters in the alphabet are R.I.P. *(Beat).* Then I shot him. *(Beat).* In his head. *(Beat).* Through his E … Y … E.'

Victor seems to find the perfect musical accompaniment for everything he does. He dances around the room as he smilingly brings his former friends to their sudden deaths. There is not an ounce of pity or regret beneath his smile. Is Victor doing what he does for the cause, or is he doing it to satisfy a deeply rooted homicidal need? In the second act,

Victor confronts the only woman who used to mean something to him. 'Please Victor. You loved me once back then, didn't you?' He coolly replies: 'It's too far off now. The love song of killing can't be undone'.

In the last act, Victor meets his dying mother in her hospital bed. You don't know whether to laugh or cry when she tries her best, but fails to understand him. Scanlon titillates you with the dialogue. Victor's mother asks casually if he is still jumping off rooftops or killing girls. Victor replies that he bruises easily because he has a deficient diet. After several allusions to the Holy Trinity, his mother gets upset when she mishears him say he's now a Jew. He corrects her and tells her he is a vegan. His mother asks if he has Kuru, a brain disease you get from eating people. He retorts, quite medically correctly: 'Kuru you get from cannibalism! Hence veganism incompatibility. Jesus!'

The final act is more James Joyce than Lecter, as Victor and his senile mother attempt to speak to each other. The metaphors and allusions become increasingly biting and complex. Will Victor kill his mother too? A mercy killing, perhaps. Or a thrill killing in the name of mercy? Will he kill himself? Is Victor's appetite for killing ever satisfied? Do human beings exist without empathy? What does Victor really want?

I have already told you too much. This is a delicious read. Along the way, you learn about the soul of a brilliant psychopath, a man without conscience, a man without fear and without regret.

Steven Simring, MD is Clinical Associate Professor of Psychiatry, Columbia University College of Physicians and Surgeons

Boys Don't Cry

I was driving Tennessee back roads in a stolen Lincoln Continental. It was black not like me. It was twenty years old. Like me. It needed work under the hood. Like me. It had 120,000 miles up and would do another 100,000 based on the heft of the engine. I knew what I was talking about. Daddy took cars and trucks apart in our backyard. And me. We could fix and steal anything on wheels. We could hotwire the fucken Space Shuttle.

Our Daddy was a hood.
But he wasn't very good.
Ah ha
Our Daddy was a hood.
And he'll never by any fucken good.
Ah ha.

We sang to ourselves. We loved Marc Bolan and T Rex. We wore blood-red lipstick when there was a full moon or for a dare.

Daddy loved random cruelty. Daddy loved the lure of easy scores. Daddy loved keeping score. Daddy loved to beat us senseless – ah ha.

He was mostly into break-ins after hours.

So he was mostly into prisons.

He tripped going into pharmacies. He dropped clues in 7–11s like an envelope with his name and address.

Me and my brother Robbie were the getaway drivers on some of his jobs. He was usually as drunk as a skunk on a lunk, Ma kept telling us although she was not far off.

We usually jumped out and ran off up the road as soon as he shuffled into the target.

I was only 12. I could not even see out the windscreen. Rob had to call out – left/right/fuck/hard right/straight/slow/fuck/stop/fuck/reverse/straight on/Banzai!

When Daddy got out of prison he drank Jameson all day. He liked to support the export economy of the Irish motherland.

Then he beat us black and blue with belts and sticks.

We were embossed with striated deep tissue bruising.

Purple and black.

Front and back.

It was for our own good.

To strengthen our resolve.

It did.

To kill him.

Not what he intended.

Another master plan gone awry.

Nothing new.

In our fucked up avenue.

On our last job together as a team he jumped from the truck in the back lot of Leroy's Liquors shouting 'Banzai!' (that's where Rob got it) – 'be good boys – be back I'll be before you know it'. Synge delusions had he.

We drove over him.

It made crunching noises.

We broke his back.

He wouldn't be back.

Ah ha.

I got out to look.

He was staring up at me as if he couldn't believe his petechiae rich eyes.

How we laughed. Ha ha.

Rob stepped down from his seat.

He bent down.

In both full father eyes he did spit.

Shakespeare delusions I know.

Then he pissed into his mouth.

– Rob I think you are going a bit far.

– Am I?

He shrugged.

I shrugged.

Blood and urine flowed out of Daddy's mouth.

Rob bent down close so Daddy could hear.

– Daddy – you're the worst criminal ever.

You're pure thick.

You're a pure fucken oaf.

Now your back is broke.

Ah ha.

Rob was precocious for eight.

He turned to me.

– I'm late for school Victor.

I took his hand and walked him there.

Five blocks.

A proper educational foundation is fundamental. School absenteeism is the scourge of the poor working class. That would be us.

Then I lurched home.

The police arrived soon after.

Two yokels with strapped pistols bright.

They were chewing gum. It could be cud.

– Is your mother home, boy?

I am not fucking Black I screamed back. In my head. I shrugged.

– You some cut of a dummy, boy?

The other cop explained about my stammer, the inbred instep.

The cop looked down at my foot. He looked away, embarrassed.

Ma appeared in the doorway smelling of cigarettes and despair at 20 paces.

– Sorry Mam, I regret to inform you that your husband met with an accident. He left the truck in gear somehow. It rolled over him. He is deceased at this time.

– What about later. Will he be not dead. I said in my head.

Ma said, the same fellow was a pure retard – he was the worst criminal in Texas. Shit what'll we do for money now?

They turned to leave. Nodded at me.

– Take care of your mother. You're the man of the house now.

– Crip – surely?

Ma could not work. She could not clean. She could not piss straight. She could not cook baked beans. She spent her days in the dark back bedroom. Smoking. Sobbing on high. The spoiled beauty queen. Choking back the terminal wailing.

Money was ok though. We had forged Daddy's signature on an insurance policy months earlier. Every week I demanded money with menaces from the local kids. I just showed them my black teeth, my razor eyes and the long knife strapped to my skeletal chest. That would do it I hear you say. You are correct.

We lived in the Aryan backwater of Shelby South. We had swastika tattoos on our pale Irish breasts thanks to Daddy. Rob was *uber* intelligent. He loved learning. Just as well. He was a pyromaniac with exhibitionist tendencies. He burnt downtown Shelby South down to the ground. He went on to Columbia University. Full scholarship. IQ and SAT scores off the charts. On moving-in day I drove him there in the truck we used for the Daddy back breaking sonata. When we arrived he said drop me around the fucken corner Victor. No offence! Brotherly love is a beautiful thing.

He graduated *summa cum lauda*. He did a PhD in Ethnography. I lost track after that.

I did not fare as well. *Summa cum laudanum*. Heroin chic – in down deep. Brown sugar and Aryan blood flow-back. A match made in heaven where Daddy prays not. It lays me down to rest. My pale Irish black soul to keep. Reminding me of something.

Ma sold the business after Daddy had his accident. I dropped out of school. No officials called round. Ma watched me from the bedroom as usual. Smoking. Camels, Salems. Praying without knowing for the cancer truck that came and ran her over. Pelvis putrefaction plowing deep. The smell was atrocious. We wore masks in bed. We burnt tires and cats to counteract the odor. I can still smell her dead. We buried her out back. We had no money for elaborate disposal. We wrapped her in a sheet and lugged her out. Her head hit off each step. She never liked the same stairs. She lies facing westward at this time. From whence she came. Huddled up now, she cries no more.

I stole the Black Continental Lincoln in Shelby North a month earlier. Shelby North is five miles from Shelby South. Some geriatric left his car idling outside the drugstore while he tottered inside to pick up pills for creeping forgetfulness. He should up the dosage. He saw me drive away. I waved at him. He almost put his hand up to wave back. They are very friendly in Shelby North.

It was spur of the moment for me. I threw his magnetic angel on the dashboard out the *fenestre*. It was obviously defective. I drove to the nearest mall. I switched plates. Then I headed east towards Tennessee.

I ate at diners every eight hours. Even if I arrived outside the next aluminum food-tube with fifteen minutes to spare I waited.

Timing is everything.

Even if spur of the moment.

See above.

Fries, burgers, toast, beans, rice, catering packets of sugar. My teeth were fucked. But it was all good. I stopped at convenience stores for water, Doritos, Twizlers, chewing tobacco, gum, jelly beans, snow cones, ice lollies, coffin nails, and the *New York Times*. Almost no place had it. I missed it madly.

So two weeks later I was driving down this dusty rural road in Tennessee, the window open, smoking, my elbow out the window. The AC was shot.

On the car radio cajun music rolled out. Daddy loved it too. He wasn't all bad I suppose. It has Irish roots. Pale Irish foreskin forefathers four generations back.

In the rear view mirror I saw a car closing fast with billowing dust above it. Then the dented silver grill tailgating. They laid on the horn heavy. I was relaxed after weeks on the road so pulled in. They kept bumper baiting. Eventually they roared past giving me handgun firing gestures out the windows with simulated recoils – impressive – shouting abuse I could not discern. I had a burst eardrum from Daddy tantrums which I neglected to mention.

A few minutes later I drove around a slow curve in the road – their car was parked askew blocking me. Three black teenagers lounged against the long hood. They looked the part. The looked like warriors. They looked serene. They looked mean. They looked supreme. Unlike the Supremes on their car radio. I stopped ten feet from them. Road dust settled slowly shrouding us.

I stepped out. Thank God I didn't have allergies. I had enough with the full fulcrum stammer. The Black-47 chic physique. The fucked foot. I was Aryan fodder truly. But I had perfect skin and fine blonde hair that fell over my blue green eyes. I had to flick it aside every few seconds so I could see them clearly now the dust had gone.

They were staring.

I leaned back against the hood.

It wasn't nonchalant pose wise like my non-Aryan brothers.

It was so I would not fall over clubfoot wise. I was in my bare feet. It is next to holiness. Touching the dusty earth and all like.

– What the fuck you doing cracker?

– Nu … nu … nu ... thin …

– Cat got your tongue stammer boy?

They all laughed. If they only knew about me and cats.

I looked down at the ground.

Cruelty followed me down all the days of my life.

– You crackers think you own the fucking road.

I shrugged.

– There was tons of room to pass retard.

– Mea culpa.

I had no stammer when I used Latin.

It rhymes I know.

I picked it up from Rob's recitation in his sleep when we lay buried from the dying Mammy smell under the shroud-like sheets.

– May-a- what-the-fuck?

– La … la … la … tin la ... la … lads.

– We're not your fucken lads you cracker retard. What's up with the foot? Holy fuck.

I pushed away from the car towards them a foot. They looked askance. They looked at each other.

– You ever hear of Emmet Till?

I nodded.

– You ever hear of Malcolm X?

I flashed them some LA gang signs. They didn't like that I can tell you!

They began to stride towards me – angry, loose-limbed, panthers. The real ones.

The sun shone off their metal baseball bats. The driver still sat in the car. He threw an empty beer bottle into the roadway. It broke and the dregs sizzled on the hot road.

I looked up into the trees that sloped down to the roadway. The canopy formed a grotto around us. It's a Catholic thing. It filtered out the killing sun. The faraway high branches swayed for me. The air smelt of heaven. Unseen critters (local lingo!) moved in the undergrowth.

I was still.

I could feel the trees and leaves.

I was nature unfolded.

I was weightless.

I was fearless.

I could hear my breath.

I could see us all as if I was looking down from the high elms.

I closed my eyes. So it would be real. Mighty real.

The boys were quiet now. I heard their bats' muffled tipping against the soft dusty road.

I opened my eyes. They were staring. The sun glinted off my knife-cradled chest. The driver called from the driver's seat.

– What you fucken waiting for? Get him.

They lifted their bats. They forgot to listen to the quiet siren thing inside of them.

I unfolded the Colt from the back of my waistband.

The metal was etched and tarnished.

Like me.

It dangled at the end of my arm as if it wasn't there. As if I wasn't there. As if this day would last forever.

Tears came then.

The usual.

From the faraway land where boys don't cry – that I try to conceal but can never forget. Rob was the same before he attacked you with a hammer, a hatchet, a crow bar, a wheel brace, a dead frozen cat.

Ma wailed but never cried.

Daddy cried blood from his ears behind Wendy's lot.

This is how the other half grieves.

The dust ate up the fat cry drops.

My beautiful black boys were quiet now.

The Colt I lifted as if it was weightless.

I could feel the vector cotangents play out slowly.

I left them sprawled on the quiet death road – I pulled the dead driver out by the hair to move their car. I hobbled back to my own.

The dust was pooled with red black blood and black boy bodies. Their eyes dead-stared at the gliding kestrels in the Tennessee sky they would never see.

NOTES

August 15: Feast of the Assumption of Mary the Mother of Jesus into Heaven.

ASU: Active Service Unit, i.e. IRA cells.

Ballymurphy, Divis and the Falls: Hardcore Irish Republican areas in Belfast, Northern Ireland.

Brighton Bombing: 12 October 1984. The IRA bombed the hotel where Margaret Thatcher was staying.

Brits: Shorthand for the British and British troops in particular.

Callow Lake: Co. Mayo, Ireland.

Coelacanth: Pre-historic fish thought to be extinct until caught in net in 1938 off the coast of South Africa.

Comanchi (Nadia): Romanian female gymnast aged 14. First female to score a 10, a perfect score, in the Olympics.

Crossmaglen: Hardcore Irish Republican area in South Armagh, Northern Ireland.

Druid: Tony award winning theatre company from Galway, Ireland.

Fuck: Used indiscriminately in Ireland by all social classes used as verb, noun, adverb etc.

GPO: General Post Office in Dublin. HQ of Irish Uprising, Easter 1916.

H-Blocks: (Long Kesh, The Maze) Prison near Lisburn, Co. Antrim, for Republican and Loyalist prisoners.

Imprinting: Observed behaviour where newly-born animals and fowl will follow the first animal they see if the mother is absent.

IRA: Irish Republican Army.

Kimble (Dr Richard): Fictional character in American TV series *The Fugitive.*

Kuryakin (Illya): Fictional character in the American TV series *The Man from U.N.C.L.E.*

MFA: Master of Fine Arts.

Mensa: Organization for high IQ individuals.

Moonies: Unification Church.

Mountbatten: Lord Mountbatten, cousin of the Queen of England, killed by IRA bomb off County Sligo.

Paras: Shorthand for British Paratrooper Regiment. They murdered 16 civilians in Derry during a Civil Rights march on Bloody Sunday.

Pearse: Padraic Pearse. Leader of the Irish Rebellion in 1916 that led eventually to the end of British Rule in 26 of Ireland's 32 counties.

Pogo: Vertical dance movement developed during the punk era of the 70s. Approximates to jumping on the spot with the arms and hands hanging at the dancer's side. The aim is to jump as high as possible to the beat of the music. At the highest point of the jump the dancer executes a head motion like heading a ball in soccer. It develops great calf and neck muscles.

Prods: Short hand for Protestants.

Social clubs: Illegal drinking clubs used by both sides to raise funds. Loyalists (Unionists) used them to kill random Catholics especially during the Shankill butcher phase.

Thatcher: Margaret Thatcher, British Prime Minster, survived sophisticated IRA explosion in Grand Hotel Brighton.

Tout: Informer, snitch.

Vegan: Eats no animal flesh or animal products.

The *Victor* comic published by D.C. Thomson from 1961 to 1992.